Sharpen
Your Mind

Daniel Scharpenburg

INTRODUCTION

I've been practicing meditation for over twenty years. I started because I had terrible anxiety problems. I've fallen off more times than I'd like to mention, but meditation has been a part of my life for half of my life.

I've taught in a few different contexts, I've been to big fancy temples, I've taught in public parks, I've taught everywhere in between. And I've taught on the internet through the Open Heart Project, but also on my own through Facebook, Youtube, and a Podcast. Lots of people are teaching in these non-traditional ways these days.

I've been called an "every-man" meditation teacher because I go out of my way to be genuine. I try to let everyone know that meditation is hard for me too, and that I'm just like you. Because I am.

I am a Buddhist and I do teach a Buddhist meditation style, but I'm not interested in a lot of traditional things. I don't wear robes, I don't bow to statues, I definitely don't want anyone to call me "master". I'm just here to be your spiritual friend and to encourage you.

With all of that being said, here's a collection of talks. Some of these are transcribed from public talks and some are simply essays I've written.

I hope this work benefits you.

Thank you for picking up this book. I appreciate every one of you.

-Daniel Scharpenburg

November of 2020.

SILENT ILLUMINATION

Silent Illumination is a formless meditation practice. The Buddhism I really teach is Silent Illumination Chan. It is a meditation practice founded entirely in the awakening of our true nature in the here and now.

These words aren't used for no reason. "Silent" represents the core of our being. Some people prefer words like "emptiness" or "no self." What's that? It's our mind before thinking. Before we think about our baggage or the projections we put on the world. We have a lot of narratives and constructs around ourselves and the silence represents what's underneath all that. There is what's been called a "don't know mind" or "beginner's mind" that exists underneath these layers.

I call it silence.

When we can engage this silence, we can gain some insight. We can see that things are impermanent and that

7

everything is connected. Sometimes this is called Selflessness, which is a kind of heavy and hard to understand word. It just means that we are part of the world. We didn't come into the world, we came *out* of it and we are connected to everything. The silent part of our mind is free from the coming and going of all our distracted thoughts and delusions.

We could say the silence is like the sky and all our thoughts and delusions, all of our bullshit, is clouds passing through. They just pass through and they're gone. We don't have to do anything except: not obsess about the clouds. The sky isn't really effected by the clouds, and you don't have to be effected by your shit.

The true nature of your mind is free from disturbance. And we can tune into that silence even when we're in the middle of turmoil—even when everything is going wrong. That silence is still there. It's not something outside of us. It's not something we're trying to gain; it's there underneath. The nature of the mind is free of all that nonsense. And I call it silence.

Illumination represents the natural function of our minds, which is wisdom. This is related to silence because it's that empty nature that allows this wisdom to appear. This is openness—mental freedom—the ability to change and liberate ourselves.

Illumination is the function of wisdom and it responds to the needs of ourselves and others. It's where we learn how to see things as they really are and have a more dynamic and clear view of the world around us. This is clarity beyond the stories we tell ourselves and our self image. It's the sky without the clouds.

The practice is sometimes called "the method of no method" and that's why some may find it difficult at first.

Silent Illumination isn't really a practice. It's rooted in the idea that we already have the wisdom we are seeking.

To compare it to other forms of meditation, Buddhist meditation is usually put in categories of either calming (samatha) or insight (vipassana). One of these is designed to help bring stability to our scattered minds. The other is to gain insight into the nature of our minds.

Silent Illumination includes both. Traditionally it's said that calmness leads to meditative absorption and insight leads to wisdom. In Silent Illumination these aren't practiced separately. They're practiced together because the truth is there is no separation. The true nature of calm is silence.

So how do we do it?

In sitting meditation we don't try to do anything. We don't need to try to force the clouds to go away. We just try to be aware of each moment. Just pay attention to the sitting that you're doing. We're not trying to follow the breath; we're not trying to keep a mantra. We're not visualizing anything. We're just being here. Be with your body sitting. Stop doing everything else and just sit. Every time you get distracted, just come back to sitting and notice how sitting feels.

Just be here.

When we sit in this way, the mind calms down and calmness (samadhi) comes. And after we do it a little while, wisdom (prajna) follows. And even if you have powerful experiences, even if you think you've made some wonderful attainment, still just come back to the sitting. This is all there is.

SHARPEN YOUR MIND

INTRODUCTION TO ZEN MIND

This was a talk I gave at a store called Aquarius in the fall of 2019. It called it Introduction to Zen Mind. I think this will function very well as an introduction here.

So, here we are. Zen Mind. I want this to be an opportunity to sort of explain what we're doing and why we're doing it, as far as Zen meditation goes. I'm going to talk about where all this comes from and where I think it's leading us.

I was offered the chance to do a presentation, and I came up with this. I could have easily done Buddhism 101, or Who Is The Buddha, or something, but I didn't want to do that.

First of all, we're going to talk about why we are doing meditation practice. I'm not going to talk a lot about Buddha except to say, Buddha just means "the one who is awake," and I'll tell a story that features the Buddha. We're not going to go real deep into that, because the truth is that this is not about the Buddha's journey, or about anyone else's, it's about yours.

We could very easily get distracted thinking about the Buddha or any other historical figure, and not think about our own journey. I think a lot of people are prone to that. With that being said, I am going to tell this story now, it's called *The Flower Story*, and it really encapsulates what we're trying to do.

The story is that the Buddha was this historical figure that people really liked listening to. People thought he was really wise, and they would just follow him around in droves and just wait for him to say something really wise so they could memorize it. That is what his life was like. One day, he stood up before a crowd, which he did often, and everybody was really excited. They were thinking, "What's the Buddha going to tell us today? Is this gonna awaken us? Is this gonna make us feel really good?" There was a lot of anticipation.

He got up there, as he had many times before, and he had given many wise teachings before. And...he didn't say anything. The story is he just got up and he pulled out a flower, and he just showed everyone the flower, and that was it.

It's kind of silly, right?

What happened was, the people were like, "What the

fuck is happening? Why didn't he give a teaching?" They're all either confused or disappointed, or upset, because they really thought they were going to get the real teaching, the real encouragement that they wanted. Just one guy in the crowd, he smiled.

That's really the end of the story, and that is a really silly story. I have to unpack it for you, maybe, but the guy that smiled, he was just there and saw a flower. Everyone else present is thinking about their expectations, or thinking about teachings they've gotten before. Thinking about what they wanted or wished for. Or feeling extreme disappointment.

And this one guy, he's just there. He just sees what's in front of him, and that's it. He's not adding anything to the situation or making anything. He just sees a flower, it's a pretty flower, and he smiles. Everybody else around is just like, "This is crap, I wanted a good teaching," and he just is there with what's happening. And that's it.

That is said to be the beginning of the Zen tradition, because we're not really like that guy who's just there. We're not really like him. Rather, we are bringing our baggage, and our obsessions, and our neuroses into every situation. That is what we struggle with. That is what we want to learn how to do, is be here. We want to learn how to be here and be with what's happening and not bring everything from our past into it.

Not to say we shouldn't learn from the past, because of course we should, but we shouldn't live there. We should be able to live here, when the time is now to live here.

If you've ever had a bad day at work, and then you go home and you're shitty to your family, that's because you're carrying baggage. That's a very minor example of what we're talking about. Really, we're all carrying a lot from the lives we've had, from how we were raised, from all the experiences we've had. If you've ever started a new relationship, and you kind of expect it to be like your old relationship, that's baggage as well. It's the same kind of thing.

One more thing I want to say is, this is also about learning how to be more genuine. As we engage in meditation practices, we start to be more real, and because of that we start to have a little bit of trouble lying to ourselves. If we're not very reflective, we don't realize how much we lie to ourselves, but once we start learning to be more authentic, we can't deceive ourselves as well as we did before.

My example of that is, I kind of have a beer belly here, and I tell myself that's genetic. To an extent, it is genetic, but of course also, I'm making life choices. That's why I have a beer belly, because I'm making life choices. We probably have all sorts of things like that. That's an example of something that I've had to learn how to face, and be real with myself and say, "Well, I'm eating more ice cream because I want to eat more ice cream." I don't have a reason. I'm just doing it because I want to and that has an effect on my body and my overall health that I'm accepting.

We are confused in our lives a lot of the time and our baggage, and our neuroses, and our expectations really pull us around and really change how we see the world. I sometimes like to describe it as like those old timey 3D glasses, with the red on one side and blue on the other. If you put them on and you're not looking at a 3D movie, you just see things don't look like they're supposed to. That's kind of how I like to think about it sometimes. We don't see things as they are, we see things either through our expectations, or through the labels we put on everything all the time. We're constantly carrying these things around, and sometimes we misjudge the world around us because of that. Also, we're distracted, and we have trouble being present in our lives.

Sometimes, even when there's things we really want to pay attention to, we realize we're not doing it. A big example of that is if you've ever been in a conversation with someone, and you really like them and you really want to have a conversation with them, but you're just in your head. You're just thinking about what you want to say, or worse, not present at all, and you're not listening to them. I think we've all had that experience sometimes, too. I call this the daydream, where we're not present and we suffer. Our reactions aren't really intentional, we're just doing things. I call that the daydream. We're on autopilot, and we just react a lot of the time.

The truth is, it's harder to make good decisions when we're just reacting. When we're just sleepwalking through life, and we miss what's happening. We lose track of a lot of things we want to pay attention to.

I've heard people say, "It feels like my child was just

15

born and now they're starting college." I think of that sort of thing. We're not present and we lose track, and life is just passing us by.

What we're talking about is training our minds so we can learn how to wake up. This is about empowering ourselves, and about clarity, as well. What we're trying to do is see through this daydream, to see things as they really are, and see ourselves as we really are. To learn how to pay attention and to live our lives in a better way.

We suffer because we're in this daydream. We make mistakes, and we make bad decisions, and we have trouble focusing, even when we really want to. The truth is that when our attention is fractured, and when we don't see things clearly, and when we think we're lacking, it's really easy to sell us things. It's really easy for people to sell us things or ideas, and that's why this is about empowering yourself, too.

We can also have suffering that spills out onto the people around us, and that's no good. We want to turn our minds so we can empower ourselves.

I'm going to tell another story. This is an old Zen story about how our expectations shape the way we experience the world. This is called The Story of Wonhyo, who was this guy in medieval Korea. He wanted to learn Zen practice, and he got this idea that a lot of people have gotten over the years, which is, "I need to go to an older place to find the more serious teaching."

He got this idea he had to travel to China, because

Zen came from China to Korea. It's the middle ages, so travelling is really dangerous, and he's walking. He's taking this journey that's really dangerous and one night he gets caught in a thunderstorm. We don't think about that much because we have cars and things, but a thunderstorm can kill you if you walk everywhere.

He's in this thunderstorm and he finds a cave to go into to rest for the night. And this is important to the story, it's completely dark in the cave. He can't see anything, and he goes to sleep in there to hide from the thunderstorm. In the middle of the night he wakes up, and he's just incredibly thirsty. I wake up sometimes in the middle of the night thirsty, too, so I get that.

He wakes up and he's incredibly thirsty and he doesn't know what he's going to do because it's completely dark. He reaches around and he finds this round thing, and he thinks, "Oh, I found a gourd."

When I first read this story, I was like, "What?" But that was a thing they did in those days, they would collect water in a gourd and you would drink it. I guess it would make the water taste good. I don't know.

So he thinks, "Oh, I found a gourd," and he drinks water from this, and he thinks it's the best water he's ever tasted. It's really cold, and very sweet, and very delicious. He's very happy he found this gourd, and he puts it down and he goes back to sleep.

When he wakes up in the morning, there's light in the cave, and he realizes that it's a crypt. There are bones everywhere. He looks down and he sees he didn't drink from a gourd, he drank from a skull with some very unclean water in it.

Immediately, he throws up, but then after that he realizes, "How powerful is my mind? How powerful is my mind that I could taste what I wanted and expected to taste, rather than what was really there?" Which was unclean water that probably wasn't cold or refreshing. His expectation gave him what he wanted. We don't think of our minds as very powerful sometimes, but they are. The good thing about our minds shaping our reality is we have some power here. We have some power to change our experience of the world.

What we're going to do is we're going to practice calming and stabilizing our minds, and when we learn to do that, that also generates wisdom. All this noise, all this baggage stops us from seeing things as they really are, from seeing ourselves as we really are and kind of learning about our place in the world.

Sometimes this path is called the gateless gate, which seems nonsensical, but it's because there's nothing stopping us. There's no barrier, and there's really nothing special about it, it's just learning how to be here. I sometimes say I'm selling water by the river, because it's really just being here. You don't need me to tell you that, but I'm going to tell you anyway. We're really just trying to put down our shit and to learn how to be in the world in a more authentic way.

We're trying to just bring some clarity and some

awareness into our experience, and to learn to see through all our baggage and confusion in order to see things as they really are. We can put aside our delusion and turn our minds so we can see the freedom and awakeness that we already have.

That's the truth. We've got all this junk stopping us from seeing it, but really awareness is what we have already.

Another aspect of this is, we also sometimes kind of think about how to be more at harmony with the world. There is ethical teaching that goes with Zen as well. It's not about sort of, "Be good because I say so," rather it's, "Be good because, being at harmony with the world around you, you're going to have a better time, an easier time, being calm and learning to stabilize the mind. Whereas if you're out there lying and stealing all the time, it's going to be a little bit harder to be calm and be in harmony with the world around you. That sort of thing kind of tends to distract you.

When we learn how to focus, and when we learn how to be present and be quiet, then we're getting space for our minds to manifest the wisdom that's already there. We're trying to see the world as it really is, without being so clouded by our judgements and labels. These things filter our reality and we rarely have a clear picture of what's happening.

I hesitate to bring this up, but I think about, for example, if I see somebody wearing an NRA hat, I immediately have assumptions I'm making about who they are, and that is not fair. That is not fair because if I see somebody in an NRA hat, I don't know anything about them. I do immediately start to think certain things, and then I have to stop myself, and that's kind of what we're talking about, too. It especially manifests in the way we judge people, and in the way we have expectations for how this person I'm looking at is going to behave. It's really a thing that drives us apart as a world, I think.

Now, I'm going to describe some practices.

I start with a practice called the Healing Breath, that just kind of centers us and gets us ready for the other practices.

Then we do a practice called Mindfulness of Breathing, which is a practice where we learn how to concentrate and focus on one thing, which is going to be our own breathing.

After that, we do a practice called Silent Illumination. Some people really struggle with this one, but it's one where we just try to be fully present and just notice everything that's happening, and not get pulled out of where we are.

I'm going to talk for a moment about how we sit.

Sitting in a chair, sit up as straight as you can. If you want to cross your legs like I do, you can, but you don't have to. If you're going to have your feet on the floor, you want to have them firmly planted, and we're going to try to keep your feet in one place the whole time. Make your back as straight as you can. If you're slouching at all, don't do that. I've always found that when I start to slouch, my mind starts to wander, and I lose track of the meditation. We sometimes think of mind and body as separate, and I want to tell you that they're not. What your body is doing and what your mind is doing are related.

Firmly plant your feet, sit up straight.

Next I want to talk about hands. There are two different things I recommend for what to do with your hands. The most important thing is that you have a plan for what your hands are doing, because if you don't, that can lead to fidgeting. The two things are, first, what I call 'the bowl,' which is hand on top of hand, thumbs gently touching, resting in your lap. Some people call that the cosmic mudra. I think that's silly to make it sound so fancy, so I just call it 'the bowl.'

The second option is what's called relaxation, and that is just hands on your knees.

I say, do whatever works for you.

Additionally, what I do is an eyes-open practice. Some people say when you meditate, your eyes should be closed. I don't say that. The one exception to that is if I'm leading an event outside, then I say, yes, close your eyes, because there's too much happening outside.

At an indoor event, I say eyes open and look sort of downward at the floor. The point is to find something to look at that's not very interesting, that's not moving, that's not going to distract us from what we're doing. I generally like to look at the floor. A lot of people recommend just sitting facing a wall and looking at the wall. I think that's a good practice as well.

A lot of people find that suddenly when they sit down to meditate, they feel incredibly itchy. That phenomenon has a name, and it's called sitting on the anthill. It's just that sometimes we play tricks on ourselves to try to resist this. That's just what that is. That said, if you have an itch, take a minute, scratch it, and then come back to your position. If we're just thinking about how itchy we are, well that's not meditating, really. If you have an itch, I say scratch it. And if you need to adjust at any time, I say just adjust. I know there are some people who are really hardcore and will just say, "Don't move at all," but I'm not one of those. I say, if you need to adjust, adjust.

To do the practice called The Healing Breath, which is a very slow and intentional breathing practice, we inhale for five seconds, we hold our breath for five seconds, and then we exhale for five seconds. I like to do this three times. I really like this practice as a bookend for meditation, so I do it at the end, as well.

It's also a practice I like to recommend for stressful situations. That is, if you're stuck in traffic and the kids won't stop yelling, or work is really challenging, or whatever. Just take a moment to do The Healing Breath, and it'll help you center yourself. I really like that practice.

For the practice Following The Breath, bring your attention to the breath coming into and going out of your body. We can either focus on the nose, the breath coming into and going out of our noses, or the alternate option to that is focusing on the way your belly rises and falls. For whatever reason, when I teach kids how to meditate, they always have an easier time focusing on the belly. I think whichever works for you. If the nose is easy, do the nose. If the belly is easy, do the belly.

The point is, this is something that's happening all the time and we don't pay attention to it, because it's happening automatically. We don't think of it as important. Unless we're having trouble doing it, then it suddenly is very important.

Bring your attention to the breath. Implementing the practice of counting, begin noting the number one on your inhale, and two on the exhale. In one, out two. The reason this is helpful is it's our anchor. Every time something comes in to distract us, like a memory or a daydream, or thinking about what we're doing later, or even hearing a sound and thinking, "What's that?" We can bring our attention back to one on the next in breath. We want to try to not beat ourselves up, but rather just go back to one. The breath is always there to go back to.

After some time, I invite you to release the breath as your anchor. Sometimes this happens accidentally, and that's okay. Instead of having an anchor, we're just going to try to be fully present with our experience, and notice everything that's happening, but also not attach to it.

If a thought comes into your mind, like a memory for example, you're just going to note, "I'm remembering," but not chase that memory to another one and then another one, as we often do.

We're going to notice the sounds we hear, and we're going to try to just notice them and not wonder, "What's going on over there?" We're going to just try to be here and notice everything that's happening.

When we do this practice, we can tend to realize that there's a lot happening.

We close our meditation by doing The Healing Breath again. Again, we do this three times.

I forgot to mention that these practices are training. They're not something we're meant to do once, but rather something that we build into our lives and learn how to do regularly. I started leading my own weekly group because I needed something to motivate me, to make me keep doing it every week, because like many self-care things, it's very easy to not do. We look for reasons not to do it.

I like to compare it to flossing, because I know I should floss my teeth and I really want to floss my teeth, but I'm not doing it. I like to think of it that way.

Now I'd like to share with you some questions from the Zen Mind Workshop event, including my answers.

"What was the last meditation called?"

I call it Silent Illumination. Some people call it Shikantaza, that's the Japanese name that a lot of people like to use, but I just call it Silent Illumination, or just sitting. I don't like fancy names that much.

"When I meditate at home, instead of looking at the floor or the wall, I look at a lit candle that I place on the floor about six feet in front of me. I find this works better for me. What do you think of this method?"

I've heard of a lot of people doing like, light a stick of incense, and you look at the incense, and when the incense has burned down you know you're done. I suppose the same kind of thing would work if you use a candle. I think that's not good or bad, if a flame keeps you present I think that's good.

I think that is why people love campfires. If you've ever been camping and you go with your friends, and you just sit and stare at a fire, that's all you do, and it's not boring. I think that's why looking at flame is especially helpful. So actually, I like that. I think that's better than closed eyes. I know when my eyes are closed, I'm daydreaming, or worse, falling asleep. I say worse, but it's going to be really restful, of course.

"One of my biggest issues is time. I have an incredibly full home life, which I enjoy, but it makes it hard to squeeze things in. Do you have a preference between doing a half hour two days a week versus ten minutes five days a week? When you're squeezing things in, what's best?"

I think shorter time more often is better. I think even doing five minutes per day is better than doing thirty minutes once a week.

"In the last meditation we did, when we were trying to focus and be aware of everything but not let it consume us, how long would you say you give yourself with the sounds?"

I describe it as like clouds passing through the sky, and we want them to just pass. You know how when it's really windy, clouds are moving kind of fast? That's what I think of. I don't think of when clouds are barely moving. We want it to just pass. If we have a real understanding of how our minds work, that is what happens. Thoughts come really fast and they go really fast, and we're on to the next one. If we don't reflect, we don't realize that. That's what's always happening. We want to think of it as something really fast that comes and goes.

"How do you separate the observer and the creator in your lives and just get to that center spot where you're the meditator and understand everything? Letting it come and go and being a part of it, and you're not being a part of it, all at the same time. How do you allow yourself to just shut down the thoughts and accept them at the same time?"

That's a tough one. We want to learn how to be really quiet and sit for a while, and if we have a lot of trouble with that, sometimes we need a longer sit to get there. We want to just see the thought coming and not think, "I'm thinking," we want to just think, "Oh, a thought's happening." That is really hard to do. We have to practice again, and again, and again, before we can really just think, "A thought is happening," rather than thinking, "I'm thinking."
I want to compare it to, I think our language is really powerful and shapes how we think, so we use the phrase, "I

am angry." Well, that's not true. You're not angry, you're having an experience of anger. When we let our language take us that route, then our anger is way more powerful because we're saying it is who we are, and we respond to that. We make it true when we say that.

I think we want to just tell ourselves over and over, "A thought is occurring," rather than telling ourselves, "I'm thinking too much." Or, "These thoughts are heavy." Or whatever else. It's just a thought passing through, and it's really hard to remind ourselves of that, but that's what we're training to do. That's why we have to do this again and again, to really learn how to just let thoughts pass.

I know when I started meditating I had a lot of trouble, I was thinking, "Oh, I'm not meditating again." I was really upset with myself. A lot of people get that way, and that's why they meditate a few times and they quit, because it is hard. A lot of the time we feel like it's going nowhere, and we feel like we're just waiting for the timer to go off, or whatever.

I do like to say it's like working out. Repetition is what it takes. We're going to feel like it's going nowhere for a while, probably. Sometimes I still feel like it's going nowhere, and I've been doing this a while. It's really just repetition will get us there, where we can start to just feel like thoughts are occurring rather than just feel like, "I'm thinking."

"How do you separate the different types of mediation that you're doing, and what kind of purpose does each one have. Like the Silent Illumination versus the anchor?"

Meditation with a focus is what's called a concentration practice. If you're following the breath or using a mantra, or visualizing something, all of those are concentration practices. It's where you have one thing that you're trying to bring all of your attention to. What does that do? It trains you in attention. If we do that over and over, we learn how to pay attention really well, and that's really good. Formless practice, or just sitting, the last one we did, is training in awareness. We're trying to train in these two things.

On one hand, we want to be able to zero in our attention, and on the other hand, we want to be able to see the world around us, and really see it. That's what the other practice is for. Some people find the one practice really hard, and some people find the other practice really hard. Personally, I find the anchor practice more difficult than the formless practice. I know many, many people are the opposite, and they find they really love having the anchor to hold on to and it really helps them a lot.

"I know you talked a bit about sleepiness, and I've read that it's bad to get sleepy while you're meditating, but I've also heard it can really help people to fall asleep. Sometimes when I meditate I think it's worked because I've gotten calmer and more sleepier. What do you think?"

I'm going to say it's not bad, but we don't want to be too comfortable or we'll find ourselves falling asleep every time. That's why I say meditate with your eyes open, because it's easier to fall asleep. Some people like to meditate lying down, I feel like I would fall asleep every time if I did that, so I tend to not do that except in really specific circumstances. I want to say, going to sleep is almost always a good thing, so I don't want to say it's bad, but I do want to say don't set yourself up for failure. Don't create a situation where you're going to be really comfortable and it's really likely you'll fall asleep. Rather, try to do the practice in a way where you're comfortable but not too comfortable.

I wouldn't beat myself up over it if I was falling asleep every time I meditated, but at the same time, I want to do what I can to make that less likely to happen. So I want to do it on a day when I'm not really tired, and I want to have my eyes open, and I don't want to sit on my couch. I want to sit on a chair or on the floor. I guess I'm sort of neutral about it though. I wouldn't say it's really bad, but we just want to be cautious, we want to make sure we're doing what we can to avoid it as much as possible.

"If you're doing a lot of meditation to fall asleep, is that going to interfere with your waking practice? Are you just training yourself to fall asleep?"

I think that if you're doing meditation to fall asleep, make sure it's not the exact same practice that you're doing to not fall asleep, because that will get certain pathways in your brain strengthened. You'd think, "Oh! It's time to go to sleep," and we don't want that. I would say do a different practice when you're going to sleep than you do when you're trying to just meditate.

THE BUDDHA AND THE TRUTH ABOUT SUFFERING

Today I'm going to talk to you about the Buddha.

I think that at times we get caught up talking about the Buddha too much in Buddhism. I think we need to remember that this isn't about his spiritual journey, it's about yours. At the same time, I was thinking about how I'm going to talk about where all of this comes from and I can't really side-step talking about the Buddha. So I'm going to talk about him, but more importantly I'm going to talk about what he figured out, because it's what he figured out that's important.

The Buddha lived about twenty five hundred years ago, give or take, and he came from a really wealthy and powerful family. Some people say the Buddha was a prince, that's not one hundred percent accurate, but his family was very wealthy and powerful. What he had was everything he

33

ever wanted, he grew up as a spoiled child. He discovered as he entered adulthood that he wasn't all that happy.

His name, by the way, was not the Buddha. That is a title. His name is Siddhartha Gautama. The Buddha is a title he gave himself, I guess. It means "The Awakened One."

Siddhartha is living in a palace with his parents and he has a beautiful wife, he had an arranged marriage, and he should be happy. He's got everything, and he's going to inherit all of his father's wealth, his father's kingdom, when his father passes away. So he should be super happy, but he's not. He's sort of asking big questions like, "Why do we exist? What's going on in the world? Who am I?" These big questions that we might wrestle with sometimes.

The story gets told that his father hid from him fundamental realities about life, that he didn't know about sickness, aging, and death. I don't think that's true at all. I think that's a fictional story that gets told to make the story of the Buddha more powerful. People might be mad at me for saying that, but I don't think that story's true at all.

The fact of the matter is, as he entered adulthood, he started thinking, "Why is there suffering and death?" That's the point. Why is there suffering and death? Why do we struggle so much in our lives? He started asking those kinds of questions. He decided that he could not stay in the palace in this comfortable life because he wanted to find the truth about these things. He was inspired to be a spiritual seeker. He explored the religions of his day a little bit and he didn't find what he was looking for there.

The religion of his day was kind of hostile to science, mean to minorities, that sort of thing. Really cliquish, and really elitist. Kind of sexist, too. All that sorts of stuff that we wouldn't want in our religion, right? He was turned off by this, so he abandoned his life. He left the palace and he went to the woods, to the forest, because he heard there were people who were practicing strange religions in the forest. He went there to see if he could find out something, because again, the religion of his day disappointed him.

He goes to the forest and he finds people living in the forest, practicing spirituality, like shamans. Like we might think of hermits you go to the mountain to see. People out there practicing spirituality. They're doing what would become yoga, and they're doing other breathing practices, a lot of strange things. He learns a bunch of spiritual practices from some different teachers out there.

Again, to reiterate, he learned from the mainstream religion and didn't find what he was looking for. So he goes out to the forest and tries to practice kind of the weird religions that people don't talk about much. And even then, although he felt like he got more benefit from it, he still didn't find what he was looking for.

So he tried a practice that involved starving himself. Sort of like staying awake for many days and starving himself to try to get some kind of spiritual awakening, and that didn't work. Ultimately one day, he just sat under a tree and he said, "I'm just going to sit here and I'm going to try to clear my mind. I'm going to try to do these meditation practices, and I'm going to just try to be fully present in my experience, and I'm going to see what happens."

This is very important, because the one who would become the Buddha, was a regular guy, just like you and me, and he just decides he's going to figure out realities about human life. That is important because our nature is awakening. His nature was awakening, and he didn't know that until he started doing a really diligent practice. We have the same nature as him, our nature is awakening, and if we really practice diligently, we can see our true nature, too. Like he did. The story is, he found his true nature, he attained enlightenment. He had lots of adventures, and lots of students, but I'm not going to go into those much.

I want to talk about his teaching now.

The Buddha is sometimes described as like a doctor. That's because he saw the suffering that we experience in life as like an ailment that needs to be treated. His original core teaching, called The Four Noble Truths, is like a medical diagnosis.

I don't usually like to talk about the Four Noble Truths, because I think that if people know just a little bit about Buddhism, then they know about the Four Noble Truths, and they might have this misperception that Buddhism is very negative, which it is not. Because the Four Noble Truths are kind of hard to talk about, kind of hard to understand sometimes, I can see why people get that misconception, and I don't like having to go to great lengths to tell them why Buddhism is not negative.

So I don't always like to talk about the Four Noble Truths. That being said, here they are.

The first noble truth is that life is bitter and painful. We could also say life is hard. Some people like to say life is suffering. That's the number one main translation for this word, which is *duhkha*, that's the original word. The main translation is "life is suffering," but we could even say life is uncomfortable. Life is filled with discomfort. Life is uneasy.

The second noble truth is that craving is the cause of our bitterness and hate. Craving. So, what is craving? Craving is wanting things to be different than they are. Not even just wanting, but wanting very hard. Being upset that things aren't different than they are. That is what leads to suffering.

The third noble truth is that there is a treatment for this. There is a way to manage the bitterness and pain of life.

The fourth noble truth is the treatment, which is the eightfold path.

I want to say, if you don't like lists with numbers, you're going to have a tough time studying Buddhism.

The first noble truth is that we have to recognize that we have a problem. Life's not all sunshine and rainbows, right? Then we need a diagnosis. What's causing our problem? Can it be that a lot of our problems, a lot of our struggles, are something we exacerbate? We make our problems worse sometimes.

I think in terms of my kids. I tell my kids to clean the basement, they don't want to clean the basement, they throw a fit about cleaning the basement. They cry, and they yell, and they stomp their feet. They're making their lives worse when they could just clean the basement. We could all just clean the basement instead of crying and stomping our feet, right?

Then, we need to be told that our struggles in life are treatable. It gets better, or it can. If we can engage the world in a more mindful and awake way, then we're going to be happier. That's what we're talking about here.

Lastly, we need a treatment plan. We need a to-do list to help us get better. It'd be hard to do without a plan, right? We suffer because we see the world through what I call the lens of, "I, me, mine." I got that from a George Harrison song, but I really like it. We see the world through the lens of this, "I, me, mine," perception and we aren't present in our experience. Those are the two things that cause us the most problems. We aren't present, and we see the world through a selfish, "I, me, mine," way. We can't solve our issues through the lens of, "I, me, mine." We have to dig deeper. We have to turn the light inward, and put aside our baggage and neurosis in order to accomplish any of this.

With the eightfold path that has come down to us, the Buddha has given us some pretty clear guidelines for dealing with our craving and suffering. He saw things about the human condition and he came up with this to-do list, and said, "If we do these eight things, we're going to suffer less." This is not a cure, it's a treatment. We're not going to completely end our suffering, but we're going to be on track to suffering less.

I'm going to go through these eight now. A lot of time, people use the word "right" for these, and I think that attaches a kind of moralistic dimension, and that's not correct in my view. In my view, it's not moralistic, so I'm going to use the word "wise" instead. I think of "right" as, "You better do the right thing," and I think of wise as, what brings us to making better choices. Right sounds really moralistic, and wise sounds like, "make good choices," which is what my mom said to me when I was a kid.

First is a wise view. That is where we are trying to learn how to put down our baggage and to see the world as it is. We want to kind of stop bringing so much of our views into the way we see things. We don't really see things as they really are, we see them filtered through the lens of our perception. That is, we're bringing baggage into everything, and expectations, and we're putting labels on things, and sometimes those labels don't apply, especially to people. If you've ever misjudged someone, you know exactly what I'm talking about, when you put a label on something and you're wrong.

Next is wise thought. We want to become aware of our motivations. We want to think about and learn about why we do the things we do. We want to carefully investigate ourselves. If you've ever had the experience where you do something kind of dumb, and then you're like, "Why'd I do that?" Or, another really good aspect of this is if you've ever been upset at something and you think to yourself, "Why is this upsetting me? This shouldn't upset me." And then you realize with a little investigation that maybe there's something deeper going on there. That's what we're talking about with wise thought.

Next is wise speech. With wise speech, there are some things that we want to try to not do so much. Gossip, exaggeration, lies. A lot of people just think wise speech is just don't lie, but it's these other things too. Lies by omission, that is leaving out information when you're talking to someone, information that they would probably want. We may think these things aren't important, but we cause a lot of harm with our words, and we create drama in our lives and in the lives of those around us. Honestly, drama gets in the way of our spiritual practice. It's distracting. Wise speech encourages us to avoid lies, insults, gossip, and bragging. Instead we should speak words of comfort and kindness. Don't compliment yourself.

Next is wise action. This is about learning to live an ethical life, so we aren't making enemies out of everything all the time. This is usually expressed in what's called the precepts, and this is my own version of the wording of the precepts. If you Google "five precepts" you can find them. This is my own wording because I wanted to make it mostly positive instead of negative, so it's a list of do's rather than of a list of don'ts, but there was a couple of them I couldn't figure out how to do that with.

Be non-violent.

Be truthful.

Don't steal.

Have honest relationships.

Don't intoxicate the mind and become heedless.

I think those are mostly common sense, aren't they? But the Buddha felt the need to spell it out.

So that is training in virtue. Virtue is very important, because if we're stealing, if we're picking fights, if we're cheating on our spouse, again, like those bad forms of speech, it creates drama. And if there's drama, we're going to be less able to focus on our spiritual life.

Next is wise livelihood. That is, we should make a living in a way that is honest and honorable. This is probably a tough one to think about. The Buddha was talking about professional killers, but he was also talking about people who sell poison, people who sell weapons, slave traders. Those kinds of professions, he said, "Well, those are not right livelihood." And we can draw a very clear line and say those are harmful, right?

If we think about it, we might think, "Is my career honest and honorable?" I don't know. That's something we could spend a lot of time wrestling with. I don't know how honest and honorable my career is. I think it's pretty honest and honorable, but some people might disagree. And that could be said of any career, but I'm not going to say we should all quit our jobs to become therapists and librarians, right? I think we've got to make a living in life.

When I think about right livelihood, I think about the movie *Pretty Woman*. At the beginning, Richard Gere is a vulture capitalist, he's taking over companies and breaking them up and ruining people's lives, but by the end he's not doing these things anymore. I think of that. He didn't have wise livelihood in the beginning.

To reference another movie, I think of *Iron Man*. At the beginning, he is an arms dealer, and he's selling arms to anyone, and he's not being very conscientious and mindful, and his weapons are going into the wrong hands. By the end he decides he's not going to sell weapons at all, right? That's a journey from wrong livelihood to wise livelihood for him.

Next is wise effort. There are two aspects to this that I'm going to talk about. One is we need to try to stop our bad habits and develop better ones. Healthy habits are mainly what I think of with this. I think of taking the stairs instead of the elevator to get a little extra exercise. I ate a salad for dinner tonight. I didn't have to eat a salad, I could have had something else. I'm trying to develop good habits and eat salad, right? It also applies to meditation practice. A good habit to have is regular meditation practice. I could veg out on my couch and watch Netflix, or I could spend a little bit of time meditating tonight. That is the difference between good habits and bad habits. Not that sitting on my couch watching Netflix is completely bad, but I should be meditating some, and I know I should be. I think of flossing, also. Flossing is something that we all know we should be doing for dental care, and most of us aren't doing it. We know we should and for no reason we're not doing it.

Another aspect of wise effort is just diligence. Practice, practice, practice, and don't give up. This is kind of what unites the other seven and says, "We need to keep doing it, even when it's hard, even when we really don't want to." Wise effort is still doing it when we really don't want to. And in that way, we kind of want to make the eight of these things into habits. We want to practice them enough that they become our default mode of behavior rather than things we're making ourselves do.

Next is wise mindfulness. That is being present with what's happening. That's how I describe it. We're stuck in a daydream a lot of the time, we're just moving through life like clouds, and we're missing a lot. If you've ever been in a conversation and you realize you're not listening, that's what I'm talking about. We want to learn how to be present, and that is one thing where our meditation practice comes in and helps us. We want to learn how to be present, learn how to focus, especially when we want to. The worst is when we really want to be present and we're not. Like someone we really care about is talking to us and we're daydreaming and we're not present. That's the worst, right? We want to learn how to be present especially for those instances when we want to. Also, at times we should try to be present when we don't really want to. We shouldn't use daydreaming as an escape, either.

Last is wise meditation. That's described as cultivating a mind that does not move. That's how I describe it. That sounds really heavy, and sounds like this is the hardest one, and the hardest one to talk about, too. What I mean to say is, what we're trying to do is learn how to not chase after every thought that comes to mind. We want to have the opportunity to let thoughts come and go, to choose how we're going to respond to the world, rather than just mindlessly reacting all the time. We can choose what we bring our attention to, we choose what we focus on, and that's what we want to do, ultimately.

That was my talk on the Buddha and the eightfold path. I hope it's been helpful. The Buddha wandered around teaching for many, many years, and then he ate some poisoned food and he died. He was very sick before he died.

One of his students was his cousin named Ananda, and Ananda said to the Buddha, "Do we have to really follow all the rules you set out?"

The Buddha said, "You can focus on the really important teachings, but the less important ones you can let slide."

And then Ananda said, "Who's going to lead us now that you're dying?"

The Buddha said, "Follow the teachings and be lamps unto yourselves." And then he died.

Some people are pretty upset with Ananda because he didn't ask, "Well, which teachings are the important ones?" He didn't ask that. The Buddha said, "Follow the important ones, the less important ones you can let slide," and Ananda didn't say, "Which ones are important?" So, some people are really mad at him because he was the only one there when the Buddha died. But, that is what it is. The Buddha said, "Be a lamp unto yourselves, I'm not going to name a successor."

LIFE ADVICE FROM THE BUDDHA

There's this life advice from the Buddha that I want to go over. I want to see if we can kind of take it from where it's kind of unrelatable and make it relatable. That's something I like to do.

This is a quote from the Buddha, it's a very simple and short quote:
"Refrain from evil, do good, and subdue the mind thoroughly."

It's because of that first one, that evil one that made me think about it. Of course, this is all advice we learned from when we were five, but at the same time we don't necessarily do it. But that word, "evil," it bothers me. When I think of evil, I'm either thinking of something silly like

Austin Powers' Doctor Evil or like a cartoon character who ties you to the railroad tracks so a train hits you or something ridiculous like that, or I think of war crimes or demons.

That's unrelatable because I'm not evil, I'm not doing those things. So I would like to submit that instead of using the word evil, I would rather it be, "Don't be a jerk." I've stolen that, that's not my description. There's a buddhist writer named Brad Warner who came up with that, but I really like it because it says things a little more clearly.

So when my kid runs in the front door and shuts it right behind him so the other kids are like, "Why did you shut the door in my face?" That's not evil. That's being a jerk. Or, you cut in line in front of someone. That's not evil, it's being a jerk. I like that a lot better than "refrain from evil."

Again, this is something that we know. We know we shouldn't be mean to other people, but sometimes we really want to so we do it anyway. So when my kids fight, what I tell them is don't be a jerk. I don't say refrain from evil, that sounds really weird. That's how it's always translated. Or "Don't perform non-virtuous actions," which I think is even worse.

The second one is called just, "Do good," which is a little better. I like to think of just being nice to people.

There's a song, "Try A Little Tenderness," by Otis Redding, and I really like it. I imagine it as people asking him for relationship advice. They're like, "My wife's really tired all the time, what should I do?" And he's just like, "Why don't you be nice to her? Maybe try that!"

We know we could do that, but sometimes we just don't want to, so we don't. Its like, "Have you tried being nice?"

There's a meme that says, "My mind says I feel terrible all the time. My body says coffee's not food, eat a vegetable, you need more than three hours of sleep." I really like it because, again, that's something we know, but we make decisions and sometimes those decisions aren't aligned with what we know we should do.

One more reference, I promise. This one is going to be far left field, but there's a superhero called One-Punch Man, and his superpower is he can get punched by any enemy and defeat them in one punch. It's from Japan, so it's weird. A lot of people are jealous of him, and they're like, "How did you get this power?" And he just says, "Well, I get up every morning, I do one hundred sit-ups, I do one hundred push-ups, I run one hundred miles, and I have a diet that's entirely protein and vegetables." And then people are like, "Guess we'll never know."

We know how to get powerful, we know how to take care of ourselves. It's the same with our relationships. Maybe I should be nice, maybe I should create harmony in my workplace and relationships.

That's where I think of "do good." How can we create harmony? How can we just be nice and be helpful?

The last one is, subdue the mind thoroughly.

I don't really like the word thoroughly, but that's what we're doing. We're training in attention, we're training in awareness so that we can learn how to focus when we want to focus on things. We can learn how to be present in our lives, because we sort of sleepwalk through life a lot of the time.

I think that's why people say, "My kid was just born and now they're starting high school." Because we're sleepwalking through life and we're missing things. We're missing so much.

It's also why if you've ever had the experience where you get in your car to go somewhere and then you're there, and you realize you didn't pay any attention on the drive. You were just on autopilot. That's kind of scary, right?

That's what we are in our lives, a lot of times we just miss things. That's why we're doing these meditations, to train in concentrating and focusing, and also just being aware, being present. Especially when we want to.

The worst thing to me is when you're talking to someone you really care about and then you realize you're not listening, because you're not here. You're somewhere else. And you really want to be here, but you're still not. I think that happens a lot.

That's life advice from the Buddha. Refrain from evil, do good, subdue the mind thoroughly.

I like the word train a lot better than subdue, because subdue makes it sound like my mind is the enemy, and it's not.

SHARPEN YOUR MIND

I'M TOO BUSY TO MEDITATE

Today I want to address the question, "What if I'm too busy to meditate?"

This is one of a few things that people often say in a casual way when they find out that I meditate. I want to be very clear, this is something that comes up in a general conversation, not usually a teaching context. People find out I'm a meditator, people find out I teach meditation, and they say either some version of, "That's so cool, I wish I could calm my mind down but I can't," or some other version of wishing they could do it, because they think it's easy for me. They think they can't do it but other people can.

I find that question very weird, but the one I find weirder is some version of, "I wish I had the time, I'm so busy. I just try to pay attention to my day-to-day life. I want to meditate but I have such an active life I can't do it."

With that in mind, I'll put on my meditation teacher hat, and I'll answer the question: how do you make time to meditate on a busy schedule?

Really, that's a better question, and the answer is, you have to make time. You have time for what you make time for. If someone says they don't have time to meditate, I don't really believe them.

I'm not going to lie to you, I've fallen off the cushion a lot of times. I'm a normal person like you, and I know I should meditate every day, and I want to meditate everyday, but I don't do it. There was a time when I did and then I stopped for a while, and then I started again. Sometimes I do well at meditating every day, and other times I don't.

The truth is, it's really easy to not meditate. We have ten million distractions all around us all the time. If you think the problem is that you don't have time, you're wrong. You don't have to dedicate an hour every day to practice, or even half an hour. Even simply sitting for ten minutes a day, or even five minutes, can bring great benefit. If that's too hard, try once a week. The point is regularity. This is when I do it and I always do it, matters a whole lot more than doing it for a long time.

Yes, it helps a lot to go to meditation group, like the one I have Monday nights, but obviously it's harder to make time for a meditation group, because you have to have time to get there, you have time to get home, you have to go somewhere. So maybe that's harder, and maybe I believe some people don't have time to go to a meditation group, but you have time to meditate at home. It's just hard.

When I first started practicing mediation, many years ago, I would just meditate when I felt like it. I would just meditate when it would occur to me. When the idea came to me to do it, then I would do it. That of course led to not doing it very often.

The thing is this: meditation is like anything else we're trying to get better at. Anything that's for our well being. It's just like going to the gym or practicing playing an instrument, or whatever. You don't get it right away and you don't get better unless you practice over and over with regularity.

The important thing is routine.

What works for a lot of people is, you either put it into your morning routine, or your evening routine. Morning routine is get up, go to the bathroom, take a shower, meditate, eat breakfast, go to work. Evening routine, whatever you do before bed. That's what you can do as well.

The other thing you can do is of course find a friend to meditate with. Make a plan, just like how going to the gym is easier with a workout buddy, meditation is easier when you aren't doing it alone. So if you don't have an ability to get to a meditation group, the number one thing is ask someone else in your house to do it with you, and if they won't, find someone outside of your house to get together and meditate.

This is a fact that some people might live in rural areas and be very far away from anyone to meditate with, but the overwhelming majority of people reading this now live 30 minutes or less from a Buddhist temple or meditation center.

They're everywhere. Whatever centers are around you, there may be something you don't like about them, and that can be something we may have to set aside. It doesn't matter if the place around you isn't exactly what you want, the point is there's a place to go sit.

If you don't have the tremendous strength of resolve that it takes to meditate by yourself in your own house, then go somewhere where people are meditating, because there's a very strong chance that wherever you live, somewhere around people are meditating.

There's advantages to both sides, of course. Meditating by yourself, you can set aside the time that's best for you and you can do it then, but a lot of people just won't do that. Just won't. You try to set aside time for yourself to do it by yourself in your house, but then you sit down to do it and you start thinking of all the things you could be doing to clean your house. Or all the fun things you could be doing.

That's why going to a meditation center is helpful to a lot of people. The downside to that is you have to leave your house, you have to set aside travel time to get there and back, and you have to be around people and maybe you don't want to socialize.

The truth is though, in a lot of places you can just go

in and sneak out. You don't have to socialize, but if you want to socialize you can.

I think there is something with most of our minds that going out and doing it makes it more meaningful to us. It's the same thing with yoga. You can do a lot of yoga at home but people like to go out to a yoga studio or a gym or whatever and do it.

Again, there's a lot of working out you could do at home without equipment, but people like to go somewhere. It can be the same with meditation.

The truth is if I'm meditating by myself at home and I sneak a peek at my phone, nobody knows. If I meditate in a group and sneak a peek at my phone, that's embarrassing, right?

There's one other option besides meditating at home and going to a center where they do meditation, and that seems more daunting, and that's just starting a group of your own. You don't need to rent a place, you can do it in your living room or in a park or something. You just have to have one friend who's dedicated to doing it with you and then create events on meet up or Facebook or whatever, and just try to get people to come. Or put out fliers or whatever.

That's what I did, I started my own meditation group. I'm renting a space because when I tried to do it in my living room it didn't really work out. I had an outdoor space that was free, but it got cold. So I'm renting a place, and it's pretty cheap. Donations don't quite cover it but they almost do. You could rent a space, too. A yoga studio or an event center, whatever is around you. Your living room is always an option; if no one comes, you just sit by yourself. Actually, just the potential of people coming will hold you accountable, too.

That's about it for today, I just wanted to talk about what we can do if we're too busy to meditate. You just have to find the tools to help yourself. Whether that be a group or creating a group of your own, or if you're one of the lucky people that just has a really easy time, all you have to do is set that routine and make yourself do it. You have that power.

THE SECOND ARROW

Today I'm going to talk about the second arrow. It's this old teaching about how we relate to our experience. The second arrow is how we tend to magnify our own suffering. The first arrow - this is a metaphor, obviously - is a bad thing that happens, and the second arrow is our way of making it worse.

My two personal examples for this are:

This one time my son threw up, and that in itself is bad. That's gross and I've got to clean that up, right? But that's not the only thing I'm dealing with, I'm also thinking, "Oh shit, is he sick? Is he going to be sick for a while? Do I have to take him to the doctor? How long is that going to take? Am I going to have to miss work? How many days do I wait before I take him to the doctor? Do I take him today or do I wait until he's been sick for two days or three days? I don't know."

And that is the second arrow, because I'm making myself crazy. The truth is that he just threw up one time and that was it, and he was fine. He went to school the next day and everything, because that's what kids are sometimes.

I feel like as I get closer to forty, now when I get sick I'm sick a very long time. When I was a kid I was like my son, "Oh, I'm sick for a day then I'm fine." I look forward to getting older.

My other example is, this one time my tire on my car started to go flat. So then I'm like, "Oh, shit." Well, I'm going to go to QuikTrip and they've got free air. Then at first I think, "There's going to be a line at QuikTrip for the air because it's free and there always is."

I get air in the tire, and then the next day, it's going flat again, like happens sometimes. So then I'm thinking, "Oh no, now I have to go to a mechanic, maybe they can patch it but probably not. I probably need a new tire. I probably have to miss a day of work because I'm going to be without a car. Cars are inconvenient and annoying."

That's what I started telling myself. "I wish I didn't have to have a car. I wish I worked next door to home," but of course I don't. So I'm struggling with all that and then I took my car to Discount Tire and they fixed it in less than an hour. They patched it.

Those are two examples of the second arrow. I had a

little problem and I actually made it way worse in my head. That's what the second arrow is. The first arrow is whatever happens, and then the second arrow is when we struggle with it and we steal our own joy.

The first arrow is inevitable. Things are always going to go wrong. There will be flat tires, always. Life's not always going to be sunshine and rainbows. The question is, can we learn how to respond better to the second arrow? Or rather, maybe not make the second arrow happen at all. Sometimes we really don't want anything in life to be less than great, so we get really frustrated and we make our own happiness worse because things don't go perfectly the way we want them to.

When something happens we don't like, then sometimes it sets all these mental processes and puts us into a downward spiral. Our minds go wild and we tell all sorts of stories about why things are worse than they really are. I think we all do that. I think we all build things up in our minds. Sometimes when we have unpleasant feelings, we also lash out.

Like, "I'm so mad I'm having this feeling. I'm so mad I'm uncomfortable." Or, "I'm so mad that I'm sad." And especially, "How dare you make me feel this way?" We get that way. "How dare you? I deserve to be happy all the time." And, "I don't want to feel that."

The second aspect of the second arrow is what I'm going to call avoidance. That is where we pretend something is not happening. That's the other level.

I really, really aggressively pretended I was okay when my father passed away. I was not okay, but I pretended I was for a really long time, and that didn't serve me very well. I think that a lot of us do that, and a lot of us have stories like that. Life is hard, and I also think our culture doesn't help us very much. We get this message again, and again, and again that just, "I'm going to be happy if I get a new car." Or, "I'm going to be happy if I get tacos." Or, "I'm going to be happy if I get Disney+."

The truth is that burying our sadness by spending money brings fleeting relief. Also, there's always new things to buy, so we're going to run out of money that way. People go heavily into debt because they're trying to buy happiness, I think.

To put it another way, our pain is the first arrow, and the second arrow is our inability to deal with that in a reasonable way. There's a concept that I like, it's called apamada. I don't usually like to talk about foreign language terms, but apamada I like, and it means "the absence of madness." I think we make ourselves crazy. I really like the word madness for what we're doing.

We have these experiences where we're getting hit by the first arrow and we just react and stab ourselves with the second arrow. That's madness, right?" We just react because we're not fully present and we're not seeing things clearly, and we can't just be here and be like, "Okay, my kid threw up so I'm going to clean that up." We just go crazy.

When we're mindful, we can choose to respond instead of just reacting. It's that mindfulness that we're working on here that we're developing. To just be aware and not go down this rabbit hole of either sadness or denial.

The mindfulness and awareness is so helpful to us because we can really learn to recognize when we're making things worse for ourselves. We can choose some of our thoughts, not always, but we can choose some of our thoughts and start to tell ourselves, "Okay, this isn't that bad, I'm going to get through this. It's probably going to be okay." Because a lot of the time, it is okay. Sometimes there are real disasters, of course, but a lot of the time it's okay.

Sometimes even if we're mindful we're going to make things worse anyway, but at least we can learn how to know we're doing it, and that takes away some of its power. Sometimes we can learn to say, "This isn't that bad," or, "My fears are ridiculous." That can be really helpful.

One of my kids - different kid, not the same one that threw up - whenever he can't find something, he immediately goes to, "Someone took it."

So what's he doing? He's piling the frustration of losing something, which it sucks to lose something, but he's piling on anger at a random person. That's two negative emotions together when it could have been just one. Nobody took it, nobody's ever taken it. We think we're not like that, but I think that if we really think about it, we probably have stuff like that, too. He's making himself unhappy and I'm trying to work with him on that, because that's no way to go through life.

That's the first arrow - something's lost. The second arrow - looking around to place blame. "Who's fault could this be?" He's adding to his struggle. I think that we all do that sometimes.

Another thing that happens is we might make a mistake in our life, and that's the first arrow. The second arrow is just telling ourselves, "I'm worthless. I'm never going to be good at this thing. Other people are better than me." Just being really down on ourselves. "I'm not good at anything, I'll never amount to anything." That's no good either.

Step one, a bad thing happens. Step two, blame ourselves or others. And sometimes, step three is just trying to get rid of it. Distract yourself, pretend it's not happening. Go shopping. Drink. Lie to yourself.

I don't want you to think that avoiding the second arrow means pretending the first arrow didn't happen. Denial is a different kind of second arrow. Really, the second arrow is whatever stops us from dealing with what's happening in a skillful way. Facing it properly. Meditation helps us see through our crap so we can see what we're doing to ourselves, and we can learn to witness what we're doing instead of just being all caught up in ourselves all the time. Just thinking, "Oh, who took my toy?"

Little by little we can learn how to see things more clearly and see through the things we're telling ourselves. We really want to not lie to ourselves, and not make things worse, and not pretend things aren't happening. Hopefully we can learn how to see what aspects of our struggle are optional, and what aspects are not. Because it's true, some of them are not, but if some of the things making us unhappy are things we're choosing to participate in, we should try to learn how to not do that.

THE THREE KINDS OF LAZINESS

Laziness is a thing that we don't talk about enough, I think. It's often something that stops us from being consistent in our practice, but also in anything else that we're doing for our personal development or self-care. It's very common, and I think everybody struggles with it some. It's a powerful force and it gets in our way and regularly stops us from working toward our goals.

In Buddhism we talk about three different kinds of laziness. We might not normally think of these things as laziness, but they all come from the same place.

They are procrastination, feeling unworthy, and busyness. Busyness is my favorite. They keep us stuck and I think that just identifying them and being aware of them in itself can help us manage them. If you can give it a name, then you can kind of take some of its power away.

Procrastination is what we normally associate with laziness. It's, "I want to avoid inconvenience. I'll do it later. I want to stay in bed. I don't want to go to meditation, I want to stay home." We can come up with all sorts of excuses to avoid doing anything. We can think, "I'll do it next time." Or, especially, a lot of people have, "I need to come up with the perfect time and situation in order to meditate." Or in order to do anything, things have to be just lined up perfectly and if they're not, then I'm not going to do it, and that means you're probably not going to do it.

Also things like, "I would meditate now, but I just don't feel like it." It's all rooted in being comfortable. I'm comfortable doing this, I'm not comfortable doing this new thing, or I'm comfortable just sitting around. I'm comfortable sitting on the couch watching TV instead of meditating. This not only stops us from achieving our goals, but it can also really limit our experience of the world.

I went to college. I went to KU, so I lived in Lawrence, Kansas for five or six years, and I didn't go to the Kansas Zen Center. I made excuses to not go there because I went there and it was a house. It was a house and there wasn't a very clear sign that I could see, so I was nervous. I didn't have a friend to go with, so I just made an excuse. I was like, "I'm not going to go in there, it's weird."

They have a clear sign now, but back in 2003 they

didn't have a clear sign, so it's just going up to a house. And this is so stupid, but we make really stupid excuses like that. Like, "That's a house, I don't want to go there." So, that's an example of procrastination. It's just making excuses, and just thinking, "I'll do it later." The thing about "I'll do it later," is it could really easily turn into, "I'll never do it." I could have started this whole meditation and Buddhism thing earlier if I had just not made an excuse.

The second kind of laziness is called feeling unworthy, and that's sort of, "I can't win so I'm not going to try."

When people find out that I do this they sometimes say things like, "I wish I could meditate, but I'm not stable enough." Or, "My mind is a crazy person." Or, "I can't settle down." Or, "My mind's too scattered, I'm too easily distracted." People say all kinds of things.

What they mean to say is, "I'm not like other people, I can't do it like other people have." We're all easily distracted, so I find that really strange and I try to tell them. Of course they don't believe it, because they think, "I'm not good enough. I can't focus to meditate." This is more common than you think. A lot of people think meditation is really cool. They also think that they can't do it.

That is the second kind of laziness. Feeling unworthy. And it applies to other things, too. It applies in all sorts of ways, rather than just for meditation. It's also not applying for a promotion because you think you won't get it. Or not asking out a person because you think you're not good enough for them. Or not doing whatever creative thing you're into because you think you're not good at painting, or poetry, or whatever you might do. That's a case of feeling unworthy. It's all rooted in hopelessness and ignoring our potential. Whatever the thing is, we should just try to do it and see what happens.

The last kind of laziness is the laziness of busyness, which at first seems counter-intuitive. It is just, "I'm too busy." I think there's two aspects with this, and one of them is an excuse. That is when people say, "I have a really active life, I don't have time to sit down and meditate." That is almost never true. Someone may not have the time to go to an event to meditate, but everyone has time to meditate. Unless you literally wake up in the morning and you're completely swamped with activity all the way until you go to bed, you can take ten minutes. The truth is, when you're using it as an excuse, it's because you don't want to do it.

I understand that. There's things I don't want to do, too. So, that's the aspect of it that's a lie, but there's another aspect of it that is true, at least kind of true. That is, in the modern world we have really learned how to fill our time. Sometimes we fill our time in unexpected ways.

One day, I figured out a way to check my phone and see how much screen time I have on there, and it is absurd. It is absurd how much screen time I have on my phone. I think that most of us are that way. It was a big surprise to me, and I think it's a big surprise to everyone. I think phones are the third kind of laziness for the modern world, because it's so easy to just be on it at work.

Recently I had to have a meeting with someone and they were late to the meeting. I had to wait around and in the old days, ten years ago, I would have just been sitting around. But of course that's not what I'm doing now, I'm sitting there scrolling.

And that's what we're all doing all the time, it seems like. So that's really the lazy busyness of our era, is, "I could sit and meditate for ten minutes and instead I'm scrolling on my phone for ten minutes." Accomplishing nothing, not really enjoying it, not really getting anything out of it. It's very silly, but that's kind of my weakness. I'm better at it than I used to be, and I'm trying to get better at it because it will just take your time unlike anything else. It'll steal your attention and steal your time.

There's all sorts of other things we could fill our time with, and forget to leave time for self-care and self-development. We could be spending too much time watching TV. I don't want to say too much, but spending a lot of time watching TV, or napping, or whatever. We could be doing all sorts of things to take us away from our development. We could probably all manage our time better in all sorts of ways.

We have to make time for quiet and just be fully present.

So that's the teaching of the three kinds of laziness. We may not think of these kinds of things as connected but they are.

ANGER AND SCREENS OF CONFUSION

I want to share a quote from you. I'm going to share from this text, *Cultivating the Empty Field: The Silent Illumination of Zen Master Hongzhi* by Dan Leighton, and it's a book I really love. Hongzhi was a Chan Buddhist teacher in the 1200's, that's the main thing you need to know.

He said, "Illumination has no emotional afflictions. With piercing, quietly profound radiance, it eliminates all disgrace. Many lifetimes of misunderstanding come only from distrust, hindrance, and screens of confusion that we create in a scenario of isolation."

That last sentence is very wonderful, I think.

I don't want to get hung up on the fact that he said,

"many lifetimes of misunderstanding." I think we could easily get hung up on that, and just be thinking about reincarnation/rebirth, and I don't want to get caught up in that. I want to talk about how our misunderstanding comes from distrust, hindrance, and screens of confusion that we create in a scenario of isolation.

We misunderstand things because we are in a scenario of isolation. We think of ourselves as limited, and as separate from the people around us. We don't always realize other people are having the same struggles we do. That's how we create this scenario of isolation, we think we're alone in our suffering, and that's not true. We're all having suffering, we're all having problems. We're all having similar problems, really. That's the scenario of isolation that we've created.

Ram Dass - who is a Hindu spiritual teacher, not a Buddhist spiritual teacher, but he's someone I like a lot - said, "We are not alone. Not because there are many others, but because there are none."

I like that. It's saying that we're all in this together, we're all struggling. We all have sickness, old age, and death. That's a very important thing to remember, and I think we forget that when we get mad at each other. We forget that we're all suffering, we're all experiencing sickness, old age, and death. Every human being on this planet, regardless of their views, regardless of whether or not they agree with us on things, regardless of whether or not they do really awful crimes. We're all struggling with old age, sickness, and death. We're all seeing people we love get old and sick, and die, and we're all getting old and getting sick and dying. We're all in this together.

It's sort of like we're in a burning building, and instead of trying to get out, we're fighting with each other about who's going to get out first. Life is like a burning building.

That is what the scenario of isolation is and, again, we make that ourselves.

We are filled with distrust because we've all been kicked in the heart sometimes. Maybe we've all been kicked in the heart a bunch of times, but we've definitely all been kicked in the heart a few times. We've all been kicked in the heart, and that makes our heart closed, and it's hard for us to trust others. It's hard for us to love others. We tend to sort of project that and think, "Well I was kicked in the heart by this person, therefore I'm going to get kicked in the heart again. Everyone's going to let me down."

A lot of the time, that doesn't serve us. When we bring baggage from our previous experience into our present experience, that often does not serve us. That's not to say we shouldn't learn from the past, because we should, but we shouldn't live in the past. We need to live in the here and now, and to do that is to not revisit bad things that were done to us in the past over and over. We don't want to live in the past, and we don't want to keep getting hurt by the same experience in the past over and over, we want to take our experience and we want to learn from it, and we want to move on.

I make that sound really simple and easy, and of course it's not, but that's what we're talking about here. We're talking about not getting caught up in distrust. We're talking about having an open heart. We're talking about practices that help us learn how to open our heart so that we aren't stuck behind a screen of distrust all the time.

We are confused, and we often don't see the world as it really is. We see the world through a filter. I like to think of those old-timey 3D glasses when I was a kid that aren't around anymore, where it's red on one eye and blue on the other eye. When you put those on and you're not watching a movie, you just see the world and it looks kind of messed up. I like to think that's what our perception is like.
Into every experience we are bringing all of our neurosis and all our baggage. We're bringing that into every experience in our lives, and we're not seeing the world as it is. We're seeing the world as we are, or as we expect it to be. That's what we're talking about - screens of confusion.

Rarely is the world what we expect it to be. If we can put down our screens of confusion and be in the present moment and just see the world as it is, just for a few minutes, I think it can really transform our lives.

Now I'm going to talk about hindrances. The screens of hindrance that we have. I'm going to talk about that as what we call the poisons - greed, hatred, and delusion. I'm

74

going to zero in on hatred, because I think that is something that we all struggle with. Maybe hatred isn't the right word, and we could call it ill-will, or we could even call it anger, I think. We think of hatred as something really extreme and that's not what I'm talking about, I'm talking about when we wish harm on another person, or when we delight at another person experiencing harm. I'm especially talking about when we let our anger get the better of us.

Is anger ever helpful?

I want to first of all say that I think our language around anger is really good. By that I mean, we often say, "I'm angry," and I think that's really reflective of what anger is like a lot of the time. "I'm angry" means that anger is taking over my being. I'm not Daniel if I'm angry, I'm angry. I'm not a person if I'm angry, I'm just that feeling of anger. It's dominating my thinking. It's making me sweat, it's maybe making me turn red, it's making me lash out at things that aren't related to what I'm angry about. It's dominating our thinking. We say "I'm angry" because anger has that tendency to just dominate our thinking and shove everything else out.

We could instead use the language, "I'm experiencing the emotion of anger." If we've got a handle on our anger, we're not angry, it's not dominating our thinking, we're just experiencing the emotion of anger.

An example of what I mean. If you've had small

children you know there are times that, for no reason, they push back. When you tell them to put on their shoes, or put on a jacket, or finish their dinner. Whatever you're doing, there are times when kids push back for no reason. And that is irritating. There are times when children push back, and I become angry. There are times when I don't become angry, but I experience the emotion of anger. When I become angry, I'm going to yell at them, and the secret truth is that yelling at them doesn't really accomplish very much. Maybe some kids respond really well to being yelled at, but the kids in my house do not. They push back harder, and it escalates.

That is unskillful anger. It is unskillful anger if it escalates. It is unskillful anger if I yell at someone and they yell back, or I yell at a child who's not listening and they don't listen even harder. That doesn't help anybody. That is a situation where becoming angry is not useful. I don't always remember that, but I try to always remember that.

I think we could have all sorts of experiences like that in our lives, outside of children. Of course we could have difficult coworkers, or of course sometimes we get angry at our significant others. That's natural. If you're around someone all the time, or you're very close to someone, you're going to get angry at them sometimes.

The question that I want to ask, and I'm wondering if we can answer is: Does it help? Does it help us?

I know I've heard people saying, "I had a right to be

angry in this situation. This person was really awful to me and I have a right to be angry."

I don't want to think in those terms. I don't think it's about having the right to be angry. Why is it about rights? It's only about, "Is my response to this situation helping me?" Getting angry - and I want to advocate trying to experience the emotion of anger rather than getting angry - but in both cases I think we can really ask ourselves, "Is this response to the situation helpful to me?"

Because it is a response. Getting angry or feeling the emotion of anger, feeling any emotion is a response to a situation. It's not about, "I have the right to get angry," because I think emotions by their nature, we always have a right to have a feeling. I don't think of feelings as justified or not justified. I think that's a silly way to look at emotions, because it doesn't matter. Feelings are not right or wrong, they just are. Feelings just are. When they arise, we can try to manage them and try to kind of have a moment to pause and say, "Is this feeling helpful to me?" Or, "Is lashing out helpful to me? Or should I hold back?"

Rarely does lashing out in anger help anyone. It almost always ruins whatever situation you're in. It almost always escalates and makes things worse, and makes you less happy. I don't want to make a huge blanket statement and say anger has never helped anyone, it would be unfair to say that. I do want to say that it very rarely helps anyone. It almost always hurts.

I think maybe when we think we're really one hundred percent right in a situation, then maybe lashing out gives us a feeling of pleasure at the time. I think that's a thing that happens, but that kind of pleasure is fleeting. Ultimately it may give us a sense of pleasure but that doesn't mean it's helping the situation. That doesn't mean it's helping anyone.

I think we need to be very careful, and I think that's why in Buddhism, anger is listed as one of the three poisons. It can really ruin things for you. You can lash out for one second in anger and it can ruin things for a long time. It can ruin a friendship, it can ruin a conversation, it can ruin a relationship. Anger can do all those things, and that's why it's listed as a poison. It's not listed as a poison because it's always bad, it's listed as a poison because when it is bad, it's really problematic. It really hurts a lot.

The truth is that extremes of all kinds hinder our ability to see the world clearly. You see what I did there? I didn't say they prevent us from seeing the world clearly, and I didn't say they make it impossible to see the world clearly. I am saying they hinder our ability to see the world clearly, and we need to have that in mind.

I think if you drink three beers in a row, it hinders your ability to see the world clearly. It doesn't completely destroy your ability to see the world clearly, but it hinders it. Probably a lot of things we put into our body do, right? If I drink a bunch of coffee in a row, it also hinders my ability to see the world clearly.

I think we need to think about that. So that we know,

and we can reflect and say, "Am I seeing the world clearly?"

I will not say it's not okay to be angry, but I will say that we need to have a lot of care. A lot of self-care around anger. If we start to tell ourselves that it's okay to be angry, we could run into trouble. And again, it's not about good or bad, we have the experience of anger because we're experiencing anger.

We have the power to learn how to have a space in between what's called stimulus and response. The stimulus is somebody doing something that upsets us a lot, and the response is how we handle that. If somebody says or does something that makes us angry, we can have that space where we think, "Am I going to escalate if I do something? Should I do nothing? Is doing nothing worse than doing something?"

We can have that space to think about that, and try to be clear headed. Although it's hard, we can try to be clear headed.

It's also suggested that anger is addictive, that it's chemically addictive in our brains. That is kind of a scary thing to think about, right? It's addictive because when we're angry, we really think we're right. We love to think we're right. That gives us feelings that kind of bring a sort of pleasure into our minds. I think, "Because I'm angry, I must be right." That's kind of what we convince ourselves sometimes. Being right feels really good, therefore it's addictive. And that is really dangerous.

I think the more we give in to anger, the more we are likely to give in to anger in the future. There are these pathways in our brain, and we strengthen these pathways when we indulge them. The more we give in to anger, the more likely we are to give in to anger. The more we create space and try to strengthen our ability to see the world clearly, and the more we engage being in the present moment, the more likely we are to do those things, too. That is how the brain works. We want to strengthen those pathways that are helpful to us, and we want to not strengthen the ones that get in our way.

Anger gets in our way. Not always, but often.

REASONS WE DON'T MEDITATE

I have this friend who said, "I really want to come to your event, but I'm terrible at meditating."

I want to talk about how hard it is to meditate, because it is very hard. I don't do it because I'm good at it, I do it because I want to be better at it. So let's talk about some common obstacles. There's a list of traditional obstacles to meditation, and they are laziness, agitation, and ill-will.

Laziness

Laziness is just, "I don't want to do it, I'm not going to do it. I'm going to find other things to do." Especially at home, it's really easy to find other things to do. That's why I like to have events, because it really makes me do it. If I'm inviting other people to do it, I've got to do it. If I'm at home trying to meditate, man, I could watch Netflix instead and that sounds really compelling. That's why laziness is, "I don't want to do it, so I'm not going to."

I think of meditation like flossing, because it's something good that we know we should do, and we don't do it. It's really easy, I think, especially in the modern world; there's so many things to do. Obviously there are many fun things that I could do, but also there's things around the house that I probably need to get done as well, and those things distract me, don't they? There's a million things that could pull us out of it, so that's laziness.

Agitation

The second one—agitation. I also do struggle with this—that is fidgeting. It's hard to sit still. Every time sweat appears on me, I want to rub it, so that's fidgeting, but also itches and things like that. We can sit and wait for those to go away, or we could deal with them as quickly as possible and come back to what we're doing. I think fidgeting is a big struggle for a lot of people. You have to meditate often, and for a long time for that to get better, I think.

Ill-will

The last one is called ill-will, and that's not something I struggle with personally, but I'm told a lot of people do. That is just, "I hate meditating." That's what ill-will is. It's just, "I get there and I sit down to do it, and I hate it, and I'm unhappy the whole experience."
I don't have that, but I think that people that do have that probably don't meditate very many times. I don't know. I'm not sure how one would deal with that.

Not only do we struggle with, "I want to be doing things," but also maybe like, "Well, I want to be distracted all the time. I don't want to be present." If we've got things we're trying really hard to hide from, things we don't want to face, then that's going to come up. Some people really freak out when they start meditating. If you're lying to yourself a lot, or you're hiding something, or not facing something, it's going to be tough to keep doing that if you're being fully present.

This is the practice of learning how to be real, I think. To touch again on agitation, sometimes I will find that if I'm moving around too much, I'll just lay down and that'll help. Beyond that, I've found sometimes that I feel fine, and then I sit in meditation and I realize my clothes are pretty uncomfortable. I'm wearing the wrong clothes. I haven't known that as I was walking around all day, but as soon as I sit down it's there.. It's crazy sometimes, I sit for a while and then I think, "Oh, my pants are really tight."

Sometimes we have to adjust what we're wearing and things like that. These things are just factors we have to figure out how to deal with. But identifying them and knowing they are present is, in itself, helpful.

THE BUDDHA'S TEACHING ON GETTING THROUGH A PLAGUE

As I'm writing this a lot of the world is in a sort of lockdown because of Covid 19.

It has claimed a lot of lives and there's a lot of uncertainty regarding when the world will open up again. And it's pretty clear things won't be the way they were before. There will be some changes. Uncertainty is scary.

The Ratana Sutta(1) is a talk the Buddha gave where he expounded the virtues of what we call the three jewels. The three jewels are traditionally the Buddha, the Dharma, and the Sangha. These are described in different ways sometimes, but looking to these things as our refuge is what makes one a Buddhist.

In this teaching in particular the Buddha is "the unequalled, realized one." He's our example, our ideal. We're looking to him as a role model.

The Dharma represents the various Buddhist teachings. In this teaching it's described as "the unsurpassed concentration that leads to awakening." The Sangha represents the spiritual community. In this teaching it's described as "the noble ones who

have understood the Four Noble Truths and work toward abandoning the first three fetters(2)"

In some places this Sutta is recited as a sort of good luck or prayer thing. It's meant to motivate and inspire.

I'm writing about the Ratana Sutta(3) now because I'm wondering what it can teach us in this time and place. I'm wondering that because the Buddha gave this talk to a group of people that were in trouble. They experienced a famine, then evil spirits came, then they were besieged by a plague. He gave this teaching to a group that had seen loved ones get sick and die, a group that faced terrible uncertainty about what would happen next...a group that was trying to engage social distancing.

And here we are.

The Buddha talked about the three jewels in order to help the people get through their challenging situation.

It's said that he had this incredible ability to see what teachings people needed and to give them those teachings, that was his real genius. So he could see someone with a really scattered mind and say "you need concentration practices" and he could see someone with very little clarity and say, "you need insight practices" and someone that didn't care about others and say, "you need compassion practices" and someone who gives into temptation all the time and tell them, "you need to focus on morality, have you tried being a monk?"

And so these people in this village were dealing with horror and uncertainty, as we all are. And the Buddha described something they could hold on to.

I'm not here to just recite the text or create my own version, but it just got me thinking about the raft. The world is like a turbulent ocean and Buddhism is the raft I'm on. That's how it's sometimes traditionally described. Buddhism is what's getting me through the struggles of life. It's my raft. And when the ocean isn't turbulent anymore, if such a day comes, maybe I won't need a raft anymore. But right now I do.

There might be other rafts other people are using. I can't speak to that because other rafts didn't work for me. I can only say this raft I'm on is really, really good. And that's what the Buddha presented in the text. It's essentially, "I see you're drowning, you can have this raft. It's has three layers. Maybe that's better than a raft with one layer."

Is this metaphor really holding together? Who knows.

When we say, "I take refuge in the Buddha, I take refuge in the Dharma, I take refuge in the Sangha" we aren't using that word "refuge" for no reason. The point is that life is hard and this is designed to help us. Life is a dumpster fire sometimes.

Learning how to see things clearly, learning how to focus, learning how to be in harmony with the world around us and have compassion for others... these are the things that bring us a sense of calm in the storm. Equanimity is something we talk about a lot in Buddhism. It's a calm and even mind when things are hard. It's not falling apart when things go bad.

I look at social media and I see people are falling apart right now. I heard about someone getting assaulted for not wearing a mask in public. I heard about someone else getting turned away from a store because the store owner said, "People can't wear masks here."

Part of the problem, of course, is that I'm looking at social media. I'm reminded of what Fred Rogers said. Fred Rogers often told this story about when he was a boy and would see scary things on the news: "My mother would say to me, 'Look for the helpers. You will always find people who are helping.' To this day, especially in times of disaster, I remember my mother's words, and I am always comforted by realizing that there are still so many helpers—so many caring people in this world."

There are people coming together that help those in need. I really recommend Dharma Relief as a charity to support

www.dharmarelief.org.

But there are plenty of other charities too.

The Buddha represents our highest aspiration. What do you want to be? I'd like to humbly suggest that the least we can do is avoid causing trouble for anyone right now.

The Dharma represents our actual course of action. What are you doing? The world has undergone a big change and in a lot of areas things have slowed down. This is an opportunity. There has never been a better time to start a daily meditation practice. Become more mindful and aware and you'll make your little corner of the world a better place. The truth is that when we train in attention and insight, we have a much easier time showing up for the people that need us.

The Sangha represents the community. We aren't in this alone. We are coming together, we have to come together. Who is your community? Who are the people helping you be your best self? We want to learn how to be a good influence and bring harmony to the people around us. That's the most important thing. It's so easy to get divided and to be divisive. Be a helper instead.

The world feels like it's on fire right now. But the truth is this isn't the first time and it won't be the last time. How can we keep it together?
How can I help you?

==========================

1.   it's called "sutta" and not "sutra" because it's a teaching from the Theravada tradition, from Pali instead of Sanskrit. Pali is a language that is almost the same as Sanskrit, so it's got words that are a little different. At times it is confusing. I went ahead and used 'dharma' instead of the Pali 'dhamma' but I wouldn't use 'sutra' for something that isn't a Mahayana text.

2.   The first three fetters are: belief in a self, doubt, and attachment to rituals. A lot could be said about those, but the Buddha is essentially saying that if we can drop those things, we're going to be happier.

3.   Here's the text if you're interested. It's not super easy to read, but it is short :

www.accesstoinsight.org/tipitaka/kn/snp/snp.2.01.than.htmlccess

"MEDITATION BUDDHISM"

The question I want to ask is "Why don't we just call these teachings 'Meditation Buddhism'?"

Or even, "Why don't we just call it the way of meditation?" We could go that far.

Although the title of this talk is a question, I don't really have an answer. But that's what I want to talk about anyway.

What am I talking about? I'm talking about the school of Buddhism that in Japan is called Zen, and in China was called Chan. It's an evolution of the same school. In the west we usually just call it Zen because the truth is the Japanese version was the first of this tradition to come to the west. That's why Thich Nhat Hanh calls what he teaches Zen, even though he's actually teaching is Thien Buddhism. That's why Master Seung Sahn called what he taught Zen, even though he taught Seon Buddhism. It just all gets called Zen a lot of the time. But each branch is a little different and Chan was the first one. Zen is essentially a word in the English language now, so it's what gets used.

What we're talking about is a school of Buddhism that appeared in China in the third century, and they called it Chan Buddhism. Chan means meditation, so really this term came about because people wanted to describe those Buddhists over there who are meditating. So we called them Chan Buddhists.

Now, if you know a little bit you may be thinking, "Well, that's what Buddhists do. Buddhists meditate, right? So, isn't most of Buddhism, Meditation Buddhism?"

And the truth is that no, there are a lot of Buddhists that don't meditate. And in the time that Chan arose there may have been even more Buddhists who didn't meditate. It was kind of controversial when these people in China practiced Buddhism and centered their practice on meditation. It's a tradition that arose to try to go back to the original practice of the Buddha. By this time a lot of people were worshiping the Buddha instead of doing what the Buddha did. They were worshiping him like a deity, like a god. Other people were doing things like memorizing texts or endlessly chanting, things like that. These things that are fine, but they weren't the practice the Buddha did. They were doing these things instead of meditating.

This movement arose in China to do the practice of meditation, to do the practice the Buddha did so we could attain what the Buddha attained. That's the point. This isn't about the Buddha's spiritual journey, it's about ours. And if we remember that it's not about his, it's about ours, then I think we're in a better spot.

What we're doing is training in concentration and awareness. We're meditating, we're doing what the Buddha did, and that is what this path is centered on. So we could just call it Meditation Buddhism. If you go to any western Buddhist community, there's a few exceptions, but for the most part they're going to meditate. They're going to teach you meditation, they're going to have guided meditations, too. They're meditators. In western Buddhism, for the most part, they are meditators. So if we called it Meditation Buddhism, it doesn't necessarily make sense. Really because a lot of these Buddhist traditions that left meditation behind, they brought it back. But also because meditation practice is the part of Buddhism that we, in the west, seem to like the most.

The meditation tradition of Buddhism, or Chan, arose in China. It was not an unbroken tradition that the Buddha passed on by raising a flower. That's almost certainly not true, but what I think is true is this. Early Buddhism was rooted in a calming meditation practice. Calming and stabilizing the mind. This helps us start to see our true selves, and when we can do that, that opens us up to the path. This calming and stabilizing meditation, when this practice was taken by teachers to China, that's when the Chan tradition arose.

These teachers of this calming and stabilizing meditation practice, they got to China and they saw meditation was really not happening. Other forms had arisen in China because Buddhism had been there for hundreds of years already. Forms of worshiping the Buddha, and forms of chanting the Buddha's name, and forms of just memorizing teachings. There was one branch of Buddhism where it really sounds like all they did was study sutras, create categories, and just put the sutras in categories. Just trying to find the best way to categorize these texts, which sounds really weird to me.

Although, it's also said the Chan tradition was influenced and shaped by some of what these earlier traditions in China were doing. A lot of Chan philosophy can be traced back to other spiritual things going on in Chinese culture at the time.

There was influence, because one of the things about Buddhism is everywhere it goes it's influenced by the local culture, and that's kind of how Buddhism has survived to the modern age. Buddhists historically have not always done what other religions have done, which is conquer people and force them to convert. Buddhism doesn't do that, in Buddhism we don't even ask people to convert, let alone force them. One of the ways it has survived as a world religion is by adapting.

When the teachers of this calming and stabilizing meditation practice traveled to China and they saw people weren't really meditating there, they adapted a little. They listened to teachers of different spiritual traditions. They sort of learned how to speak the language of the people in the area where they were, because Chinese culture and Indian culture are very different.

It's said that there was a teacher named Bodhidharma, and he specifically was the first one, he traveled from India to China to teach. He discovered the Buddhists there not meditating. He dedicated himself to encouraging meditation practice, to bringing this practice to people who never even did it before. But he did something else, too, and that is he showed them how to do the practice. He went around teaching and he showed to everyone that would see. He also taught a key Buddhist concept, and that is Buddha nature, or that is that wakefulness is part of our nature. We can all attain enlightenment.

Why that's important is because it reminds us that everyone has this wakeful nature, and because we all have this nature, no one's left out. We can all attain enlightenment, this is for everyone. It's not for some select few people, it's not for the people that have enough time to dedicate all of their lives to meditation, it's not just for the people that have enough wealth to give lots of offerings or build many statues and temples. No. It's your true nature, and it's for everyone.

That was the message that Bodhidharma carried with him. That and, "You guys should just sit and meditate."

There's a story about him sitting in a cave and practicing for nine years, and I'll save that for another time, but there are stories like that of him doing incredible things. It's said that he invented tea. The point is, the important thing he did was he taught people about our awakened true nature, and he showed people how to sit and meditate.

A lot of what's in the Chan tradition really just goes back to Bodhidharma's teachings. A lot of the other teachings are really just commentary on what Bodhidharma said. He was a really important figure. He's semi-mythical, but a very important figure and probably someone that did exist.

There are four key concepts to the teaching that Bodhidharma and the earliest meditation teachers in China taught. These four key concepts are: faith, understanding, practice, and realization.

First of all, faith. When I talk about faith, you probably have things appearing in your head because we have baggage around this word, but we're talking about faith in ourselves. We're talking about believing we can do this, and believing that this path is doing something good for us. That's the kind of faith we're talking about. We're not talking about faith in spirits, or faith in god, or life after death, we're talking about really faith in ourselves, and to an extent, faith that the path is doing us good, because it is. If we don't have faith in ourselves, or if we don't believe in the path all the way, then we're probably not going to be that diligent in our practice.

Second is understanding. Understanding is more philosophical. It is studying, learning about where these teachings come from, learning about how these teachings go together, why we're doing this. That's what understanding is.

Practice is putting our belief into action. Without practice, we could just be philosophers, we could just be people that think Buddhism is really cool, and learn a lot about it, and read everything about it, and not really do it. We could do that, and definitely some people do that. Sometimes I'm guilty of that. I love to study Buddhism a lot. I've probably spent more time studying than practicing.

Last is realization. Realization is enlightenment. It's learning how to move through the world in a more awakened way.

Without faith we won't understand, without understanding we won't practice, and without practice we're not going to realize our true nature. So these four things taken together create the path.

Practice involves meditation which can be uncomfortable, boring, and even painful. We calm the mind with meditation practice, and when the mind is calm, things become clear, and when things are clear, then we can lessen the hold of these delusions and neuroses that are dominating our lives.

That's what this is all about. It's about overcoming our delusions, it's about seeing clearly, it's about calming the mind. It's about all of these things. That's really what we're trying to do here.

So, maybe I do have an answer. Why don't we call it Meditation Buddhism? It sounds like that would be easy. But it's more than that. We're not meditating just to make our minds a little bit sharper, we're not meditating to suffer just a little bit less. We are taking as our goal learning how to live in a more awakened way. We are meditating to awaken.

I hope I've shed some light. It gets so confusing, the words Chan and Zen.

I once had someone say to me that they were turned off when they started to hear us talking in foreign words. She said, "Can we get beyond that?" Can we get beyond throwing out foreign words? Because maybe it does turn some people off, maybe it does scare some people away. I think the word Zen has almost stopped being a foreign word. You say the word Zen and people kind of have an idea of what you mean, but they may have some incorrect assumptions about it. They may kind of have an idea, whereas other words like Chan? Chan kind of has a way to go.

That's why a lot of teachers are just going to use the word Zen, and that's why most of the time I just use the word Zen, because people know it already.

I'm not ready to just call it Meditation Buddhism, but that is something I'm contemplating, because that is what Zen means. It means meditation. That is what Chan means, it means meditation.

This is the path that makes meditation the central focus.

GRIEVING AND DEATH

I wanted to write about grief and death today.

Some asked me to talk about this, so I'm going to. It's going to get a little personal too.

This is about grief and death. Ultimately an aspect of this is going to be very personal because of my own experience, and I'm going to relate that to you, but I'm going to start by sharing a quote.

This is from a book called *Awake in the World*, by Michael Stone. He is a Buddhist teacher, and he happens to have died a few years ago. In his book, he has a passage on death that I wanted to start with.

He says, "In death there is a kind of shift. One thing

ceases and another thing starts. Of course, we're not functioning anymore as the wave in the water, we become the water completely. We move back into the elements. In death, we give completely until we are not functioning relative to the whole; we are the whole. Coming and going, like life and death, are irrelevant phases when we are fully in our lives. The sunset does not die, it becomes a sunrise somewhere else."

I really like that. I think he's challenging us to think of death in a different way. Death is obviously a fundamental part of life, and we know that most of, or maybe our whole lives. At least as soon as we start learning things, we learn about death. We spend a lot of time avoiding the subject, or we spend some time pretending it's not happening, because it's sort of scary. Right? I think it's one of these human universals, it's one thing that we have in common with everyone else on this planet. We're all getting older, we're all getting sick, and we're all going to die.

And in addition to that, we're also all losing our loved ones. Every one of us is losing our loved ones, and that affects us in several ways. The one obvious way is of course if a loved one dies, we miss them. The secondary way is, when a loved one dies, it's kind of like a part of our future dies, because our potential future where we were going to interact with them is gone. We have a new future that's completely independent of this other person because they're not going to be in our lives.

I think we really struggle with that, and maybe we

have trouble putting a name on it, but that's what it is. It's a potential future going away. Even if there are times when we lose someone that we're not even all that close to, we still have a lot of grieving to do. That happens all the time. Again, that's because of that potential future. Even if we don't see someone a lot, we were probably going to see them and have some interactions. Any opportunity is gone.

To a degree, that functions in other things as well. I think when you get a divorce, or when someone moves away, a potential future is gone, but it doesn't have the finality of death.

I'm going to share with you something personal now, and that is this:

When I was fourteen years old, my father was diagnosed with stomach cancer. They attempted surgery to take his stomach out, and when they cut him open, they discovered that the cancer was too widespread. There was no chance of defeating it by taking his stomach out. Taking his stomach out was going to be a greater risk than just leaving it in and blasting him with chemicals. So that's what they did.

They left his stomach in, they sewed him back up, and if you know anything about cancer, that's kind of a pretty common thing that happens. So, they sent him home and they got him aggressive chemotherapy. I was fourteen years old, I don't know if it was stage four or stage three, but that doesn't matter for the story. What matters is he remained with us for eleven months. Then he fell into a coma, and then he died.

My dad was gone, and my brother was away at college, so it was just me and my mom in the house at that point. The fact is that at that time and for many years after, I didn't have the tools of meditation practice that I have now, and I didn't know how to talk about impermanence. I didn't know how to talk about any of this, and that's going to come into play later in the story.

My mother had no idea how to handle it, and had no idea how to help me. I have a childhood friend named Jason, and my friend Jason's dad also lost his father when he was young. So, my mother had this guy - his name was Bill Downing - come and just talk to me about his experience of him losing his father. He didn't ask me any questions, he didn't ask me to share, he just told me about his experience. And that really helped me.

I think it's really helpful to us when other people tell their stories, at least I hope so, and that's why I'm telling you my story now. Because Bill Downing told me his story of losing his father at a young age, and it made it a little bit easier for me to take. As easy as it could be. The most memorable thing he said to me was this: when he lost his dad, he didn't cry. He felt sort of numb, instead of what he expected, which was to feel devastated. He just felt sort of numb, like the world was in black and white. That resonated really well with me, because that's what I felt. I didn't cry when my father died. I just felt sort of numb, it felt more unreal than tearful.

We'll move forward in the story a little. I went through high school without a dad.

After high school I went to Johnson County Community College. My first year in college, my mother was diagnosed with lung cancer. She had been a smoker in her earlier life, for many years. She had quit smoking before she got lung cancer, but I guess she quit too late. They said it was inoperable.

So, really it was the same thing. Her treatment wasn't exactly the same, but she got heavy treatment - chemotherapy and radiation, I think. She also had an oxygen tank, a big square thing that went in our living room and it's got cords that went in her nose. Really long cords so she could go anywhere in the house, but she was hooked up to this thing all the time when she was home.

I have a really big memory of one night when the machine suddenly stopped working, and we had to call, and a guy had to come make an emergency visit to come check on it and fix it. By the time the guy got there it had come back on. So it was really embarrassing, but it's a really vivid memory in my mind.

Less than four years apart. My dad died, my mom got cancer, my mom died. There I was, nineteen years old, first year of college. I didn't know what I would do with my life. I didn't feel ready to be an adult. But there I was. Now my parents have been gone from my life longer than they were in it.

My mother had planned for this, so she set up a trust fund for the life insurance money to go into so I could finish college and have that paid for. That was very nice and that had an impact on my life. But I was just a wreck. I didn't know how to talk about it. I didn't have a breakdown, I didn't explode, I was just numb, and sad. I felt broken. I really struggled in college, I almost dropped out because my grades started slipping because I was just sad.

So I went away to college, I went to KU, the University of Kansas. I think people that know me from that period, especially people that have not known me since really, probably would see me as a very sad, very irritable, very depressed all the time, morose person. That is who I was. I was a very negative and pessimistic person because I was carrying all that weight. It's only in more recent years that I've learned that about myself. It deeply affected a large part of my life for a long time. It really had an effect on me. It really made me a negative person, and I've only become a positive person recently.

Some people say that college was the best time of their lives. That was not my experience. I was just grieving the whole time, or at least most of it, and that grief sort of infected all of my relationships. It was always there, I was always grieving and struggling. I didn't have anything to help me get through it. I tried therapy two times, and both times I was not willing to open myself and talk. I struggle with talking to someone I just met anyway, but I was not willing to open myself and talk, so I think therapy was always going to be a struggle.

That's my story. I didn't have any tools to deal with that. I sometimes wonder if I had meditation practice, if I had training in attention, if I had the Buddha's teachings on impermanence - would I have had an easier time? I tend to think I would. I tend to think, "I wish I knew then what I know now."

Like I said, the most helpful thing to me was Bill Downing came to my house and just talked to me about his dad, and how his dad had died. That helped me because it made me feel like I'm not alone, because his experience was like mine. The truth is, none of us are alone. None of us are alone, we're all dealing with this exact thing. People we love die. People we love die, and then they're gone, or at least it feels like they're gone.

I could give you an answer that says, "We can take comfort in this, or we can take comfort in this," but I really wanted to tell my own story before I do that.

We can take comfort in a few things. One is reminding ourselves that we're not alone, we're all in this together. I wish we would remember that when we feel like being mean to each other. I think that when we have conflicts with other people, it's sort of like having a fight inside a burning house. We're in it together, we're burning together.

We're all burning.

There are diverse views on this. Some people like to say that when you die your spirit goes somewhere else, or when you die your spirit's born again, and things like that. I have no opinion on the subject. I don't. What I know is that when you die, I don't see you anymore. However, that said, there's another way we can think about this.

I'm going to share a quote from another book. This is called *No Death, No Fear* by Thich Nhat Hanh. If you're struggling with death or grieving, this is a book I recommend for sure. He wrote this about when his mother died.

He wrote,
"Walking slowly in the moonlight through the rows of tea plants, I noticed my mother was still with me. She was the moonlight caressing me as she had done so often, very tender, very sweet. Wonderful. Each time my feet touched the earth, I knew my mother was there with me. I knew this body was not mine, but a living continuation of my mother and my father, and my grandparents, and great grandparents. Of all my ancestors, those feet that I saw as my feet were actually our feet.
Together my mother and I were leaving footprints in the damp soil. From that moment on, the idea that I had lost my mother no longer existed. All I had to do was look at the palm of my hand, feel the breeze on my face or the earth under my feet, to remember that my mother is always with me, available at any time."

I think that says a lot, and I wish I had a book like

that, I wish I had access to teachings like that when my father passed away and when my mother passed away. If I'm really honest about my journey, I do think losing my parents led me to become a seeker, which led me to doing this thing I'm doing now. I see a direct cause and effect relationship there.

So, what is he saying? He's saying his connection to his mother, thinking about that connection, reminds him that she's not really gone. If we shift our thinking, we can come to understand - no one is ever really gone. That's really hard to tell ourselves.

In the case of my parents it's very obvious. My parents came together and they created me, I have a lot of their traits. I have their genetics, right? But I think it applies even beyond that. I think that the people we interact with help shape who we are. That doesn't just apply when we're forming, when we're young in our formative years, but really other people influence us all the time. For good or ill, we're shaped by other people. We are shaped by big interactions and by little ones. In that sense, no one's ever gone.

In the Michael Stone book I referenced earlier, he said, "We're not waves anymore, we're the water." That is a common way of describing human beings in Buddhism, no self. Our identity is not as solid as we think it is, we tend to think we're separate from everything else. There's a description of people in

Buddhism as waves in the ocean, so the ocean is everything and we are waves. We come out of the ocean, we exist for a while, and then we're gone. But we're always part of the ocean, we're never really separate from it. We just tend to think we are, and we tend to think other people are.

We're all part of the same whole. If we can think of that, if we can shift our minds and think of connectedness, connection, interbeing, the way we all influence each other and relate to each other. If we can turn our minds on that and reflect on that, I think that can help us with our grief. We've just got to remember that if you're thinking about them, if you're thinking about someone and how they influenced your life and how much you love them, and events you shared, then they're not gone. They're not gone, because no one ever goes.

No one ever goes.

SPIRITUAL FRIENDSHIP IS THE WHOLE WAY

Ananda went to his cousin, the one we call the Buddha.

Ananda was the Buddha's assistant, so he was around all the time. That's important to the story, just to say that Ananda heard essentially everything that the Buddha said.
So, one day Ananda went to his cousin, like I said. And Ananda said,
"I think spiritual friendship, sangha, is half of the spiritual path. It's so important to our journey."
And the Buddha replied, "Ananda, spiritual friendship is the whole way. Find refuge in the sangha." *

I remember when I first heard that story and it has really stuck with me. Spiritual friendship is the whole way. Could that be true? I think we can reflect on this a lot.

When I first learned about Buddhism, many years ago now, it really spoke to me on a deep level. It was like "This is what I've always needed." I got to some of the teachings around sangha and I wondered if I could put that aside.

I didn't want to, like, go meet people and stuff. I thought I was too introverted, that I had too much anxiety, that I didn't know how to talk to people and express myself. In other words, I had excuses.

Eventually I did do it.

Who knows why, but it's an aspect of humanity that we feel weird about going to things.

If it's people we don't know, it's hard for us to do it, especially to do it alone. "I want to do this thing, but I need to find a friend to go with me," is a very strong thought a lot of people have. Whether it's attending a meditation event, going to the movies or taking a cooking class. Even people who don't seem to have problems with anxiety still stick to this rule a lot of the time.

So, there are many, *many* people that are interested in Buddhism that aren't finding their way into communities to meet like minded people. I have no idea what sanghas can do about that. I hear a lot about how these communities are struggling to get people to show up and to get them to keep showing up. I don't have any answers to that. I think these problems are complex and probably impacting other spiritual paths in similar ways.

.

But why is it so important, anyway? Can we do this alone?

Other people supporting and encouraging us in our practice is good. But I think it runs deeper than that. I think being around other people who are committed to mindfulness and compassion is automatically good for us. It helps, inspires and encourages us. And if we can actually make friends in a community, that's even better. But, really just having one friend who's interested in doing this kind of journey with you is the most important thing.

I don't know how people make friends as adults, really. But I know this. Most of our lives we have made friends based entirely on proximity—someone we met in our neighborhood, or school, or work.AND the people we spend time with influence us in ways we're unaware of.

So is having a sangha important? Do we need to go to a temple?

I don't know. But I think spiritual friends do us a world of good. Surround yourself with people who have the same goals and values that you do. If you're not doing that, why not? And if it's hard, can you find ways to do it anyway? I think you can.

===
================

*paraphrased from the Upaddha Sutta
www.accesstoinsight.org/tipitaka/sn/sn45/sn45.002.than.html

PAPER AIRPLANE

A few months ago I took my seven year old stepson to meditation with me. I don't take kids to meditation unless they ask to go. I'm sure there are plenty of people out there that would NEVER take a child to a meditation event and I do understand that. But I believe that, as mindful parents, we should share the practice with them if they're interested. Some people believe kids can't really get much benefit from meditation practice and I really disagree with that. A long time ago I used to teach meditation to kids. Sometimes I think about doing that again.

Anyway, he was determined to attend. I don't know why. There are four children in our house and he's the only one that seems interested. He has gone in the past and (to my surprise) participated in the whole meditation. An hour of sitting still is a long time for anyone, if we're honest.

But, although he really wanted to go, he also brought some activities. He said, "Just in case I get bored." He brought some Dogman books and a notebook for writing and drawing.

I wasn't leading the practice. I had invited a zen monk named Thich Tam Cu to come lead for the night. He did a great job, by the way. So, I had the opportunity to just be a participant in the meditation practice, instead of leading.

Thich Tam Cu is someone I don't know very well. He's from the American South and many years ago he was in the United States Navy. He's a Zen monk and hospital chaplain now. He's student of Sunyananda Dharma who, a long time ago, was once my teacher. He's been studying with him way longer than I did and is still studying with him today.

Whereas I decided a long time ago to take my teaching in a non-traditional direction, Thich Tam Cu did the opposite. He wore a yellow robe when he led meditation, because he wears robes when he teaches. He's actually not as traditional as I thought he would be, but more traditional than I am. He uses humor just like I do, which I didn't expect.

It seems like I swear and talk about memes, drinking, and how fucking hard it is to start and maintain a consistent meditation practice in all my dharma talks. Not traditional, a little different. I'd rather be your friend and inspire you than be your teacher.

Anyway, what I discovered was that his style is similar to mine. That time I spent training with his teacher may have had more influence on me than I realize. Who knows.

Maybe 'traditional' is just a word I'm attaching importance to that isn't there. I'm probably not as different as I think. If I'm honest, for a second there I thought to myself, "Maybe I should get the robes out of the back of my closet…"

I was there and we were sitting, doing a very similar practice to the one we do when I lead, presented by this monk in a very similar way to the way I present it. 30 minutes of meditation, just like we do when I lead.

My stepson sat with me a few minutes. Then he left to go across the room where he had his bag full of activities. It's a big room, he was pretty far away.

We were sitting there doing the practice and I heard this ripping sound. Paper getting slowly pulled out of a notebook. Then, I heard some other sounds. He made a paper airplane and he was throwing it. He was, however, still being quiet, as quiet as one can be when throwing a paper airplane.

At first I thought, "Why the hell is he throwing a paper airplane? He knows what we're doing here! He's going to bother everyone." I was not mad, but I was irritated. And I decided, since we were meditating, to bring attention to that irritation.

And I realized two things.

First of all: No one cared but me. No one even noticed.

AND

He's seven years old. He far exceeded all expectations for a 7 year old boy, as far as not bothering anyone. Between the meditation and the discussion (which was a Q &A) we sat there for an hour. That's a long time for a kid to be quiet and all he did was make a paper airplane. (!)

And that's when I found equanimity. In truth, I was only irritated for a moment. A moment was all I needed. That's what meditation really gives us, I think. A little extra space between thoughts, or between stimulus and response, or a chance to reflect mindfully and stop a growing irritation. This is something that happens to all of us often. Some nonsense thing happens and we make it a bigger problem in our minds that it really is. We get bothered by so many things. The poet Charles Bukowski said, "We are flattened by trivialities, eaten up by nothing." I really like that quote.

Would I have found equanimity if I wasn't meditating at the time? I don't know. Everything was quiet so it was really easy for me to hear the crafting of a paper airplane. In a more active day-to-day situation I may not have even noticed, and I wouldn't have had that expectation that I was putting on him to be quiet. And the expectation I was putting on the room to be a quiet place.

The truth is that in meditation we're learning how our minds work. We're learning to see those gaps between thoughts. And when we learn how to do it on the cushion, the hope is that we strengthen those pathways in our minds so we can also do it when things happen off the cushion. The training we get in meditation is supposed to help us when we're not meditating.

Otherwise, why are we doing it?

So, that's my story.

A real and personal lesson. The gaps are really important. The space between thoughts. If we can get handle on that, we'll be a lot happier.

ABOUT THE AUTHOR

Daniel Scharpenburg is a meditation teacher in the Chan Buddhist Tradition. In his day job he's a union labor activist.

Daniel specializes bringing meditation practice and Buddhism to people in a practical way that applies to real life. He teaches in groups and retreats.

Daniel has been practicing Buddhism and meditating for over twenty years and has practiced with many different teachers. He was given teaching authorization in the Lay Chan Lineage by the International Chan Buddhism Institute.

Daniel lives in Kansas City, Missouri with his wife, four kids, and two cats.

Go to meditationwithdaniel.com for more information.

RECOMMENDED READING.

Awake in the World: Teachings from Yoga and Buddhism to Live a More Engaged Life.
By Michael Stone. Shambhala Publishing

No Death, No Fear: Comforting Wisdom for Life.
By Thich Nhat Hanh. Riverhead Books.

Don't Be a Jerk and Other Practical Advice From Dogen, Japan's Greatest Zen Master.
By Brad Warner. New World Library

Perfectly Ordinary: Buddhist Teachings for Everyday Life.
By Alex Kakuyo. Independently Published.

Buddhism for Dudes
By Gerry Stribling. Wisdom Publications.

SHARPEN YOUR MIND

www.ingramcontent.com/pod-product-compliance
Lightning Source LLC
Chambersburg PA
CBHW061148040426
42445CB00013B/1607